T
SYNOPTIC
GOSPELS

A COMMENTARY FOR
TEACHERS AND
STUDENTS

D. B. J. Campbell
Dip. Theol. (London)

Foreword by
Adam Fox, D.D.
Canon of Westminster

JOHN MURRAY

Printed in Great Britain by
Cox & Wyman Ltd, London, Fakenham and Reading
and published by John Murray (Publishers) Ltd
50 Albemarle Street, London W.1

Foreword

I had the opportunity of discussing this book with Miss Campbell when it was in process of making, and I felt at once that it was likely to prove unusually useful. It gathers together a great deal of information and commentary which must otherwise be delved for in many books, and all this is arranged judiciously and on practical lines; the author's outlook might be described as one of liberal commonsense.

I should have welcomed the book warmly in my teaching days because:

(*i*) it would have given me something interesting to say about any passage from the first three Gospels;

(*ii*) it would often have suggested to me where to begin my own preparation of a lesson or what was to be the main point of it;

(*iii*) if I had been preparing a lesson in haste (and who does not sometimes have to do this?) I should probably have found enough material here on which to base my whole lesson;

(*iv*) it would often have helped me to answer intelligent questions from my class.

Nor do I think it should be only in the teacher's hand. Many senior boys and girls and older people trying to get hold of what the Gospels say and what Jesus taught would find it valuable to have a copy of their own. I should not be surprised if 'Campbell's *Synoptic Gospels*' became a familiar sound in school and out of it.

ADAM FOX

Preface

This book attempts to sum up the conclusions of Biblical scholarship in a readable form. The writer has tried to approach the Gospel records constructively, to state fairly the problems involved and to make due mention of conflicting theories. The commentary is intended particularly – but by no means exclusively – for those beginning, or directing, a course of study in the Synoptic Gospels with an examination, such as the G.C.E., in view.

The book follows the main pattern of the life of Jesus, and brings in the Gospels as they throw light upon it. Since Mark is the basis of the others, and needs to be known in any study of the others, Mark is dealt with first. Except where the context makes it otherwise plain, the terms Matthew, Mark, and Luke, are used throughout to denote the Gospels as we have them, rather than their authors.

Contents

HEALING AND TEACHING

The Gospel Documents

1 · The Synoptic Gospels

The Gospels of Matthew, Mark and Luke, are called synoptic because they look at their subject from the same point of view. Although each is distinctive, all offer an historical account of the life and teaching of Jesus, and have much information in common. The Fourth Gospel, on the other hand, is not so much historical as theological, and so is very different in style.

For a number of years after the resurrection of Jesus no attempt was made to write a life of Jesus because people who had known him were able to give first-hand information from their own personal experience. Furthermore, the first Christians were far too busy preaching the Gospel of Jesus to stop to write it down, and, since they believed that Jesus would soon return, saw no point in doing so.

As time went on, however, and Jesus did not return, attempts were made to produce some written records. The first verses of Luke's Gospel tell of these. Only a few of such writings now survive. The four in the New Testament did so probably because they were the best. The earliest of our surviving Gospels, that of Mark, is usually thought to have been published about A.D. 65.

This does not mean that when attempts were made at records the writers had only far-off memories to help them. The years between the resurrection and the first Gospel writings were full of activity. Like other Jewish rabbis, Jesus often taught his disciples to learn by heart, and in verse form. These teachings would be handed on in the same way by the apostles to their converts, and without alteration. Similarly, stories of Jesus would be told and retold very accurately. People in the East are noted for their good memories. This is possibly due to the centuries-old scarcity of books.

In addition to this constant repetition, converts before baptism were required to learn by heart a set form, or summary, of the main events in Jesus' life. For example, Paul, himself a convert, said to his own

1

converts in Corinth *I delivered unto you first of all that which also I received* (I Corinthians 15³), (cf. Romans 6¹⁷, I Corinthians 11²³, II Timothy 1¹³, 2²).

There were also, previous to the Gospel writings, letters from one Church leader to another, or to a Church congregation. Many of these Epistles have survived. They tell us much about the nature of the Christian Faith in this intervening period.

Furthermore there is evidence of there having existed at this time written summaries of some of Jesus' sayings, and collections of proof-texts from the Old Testament used by Christian teachers in relation to incidents in the life of Jesus as and when they seemed appropriate.

All this material, together with the first attempts to write a life of Jesus, was available as a source of information for the writers of the New Testament Gospels. They made use of it, as modern reporters do, with variations according to the public each was writing for.

2 · Approximate Date Chart

A.D. 29 or 30	The crucifixion, resurrection and coming of the Holy Spirit
	The stories and teaching of Jesus repeated orally by missionaries and converts
A.D. 40	Written collections of Jesus' sayings
	Written collections of Old Testament proof-texts
	Early creeds, or summaries of the Faith, learned by converts before baptism
A.D. 50	Epistles written
	Early attempts at writing the life of Jesus
A.D. 64 or 65	The Gospel of Mark

3 · The Synoptic Problem

Close examination of the Synoptic Gospels reveals that they have much material in common. When three authors are writing of the same events some similarities are to be expected, but not word for word similarity, which is what is to be found here. The explanation must be that the three authors used the same sources of information, either oral or written, or both.

One such written source made use of by Matthew and Luke is evidently Mark's Gospel. About ninety-five per cent of Mark is found in Matthew and Luke. Nevertheless, if all the material borrowed from

Mark is removed from Matthew and Luke, there is still a considerable quantity of material that remains common to both. The conclusion from this is that, besides Mark, there was available to Matthew and Luke another source. This no longer exists on its own, nor does its name. It is referred to, therefore, as Q, because *Quelle* is the German word for source. Presumably it was in writing, because Matthew and Luke usually follow the same order in using it.

When all the material from both Mark and Q is removed from Matthew and Luke, there remain Matthew's and Luke's own contributions to their Gospels, derived from their own personal sources. Matthew's particular collection of information is referred to as M, and Luke's as L. Both M and L are composed of other earlier sources. Each Gospel has therefore three main sources.

Mark	Q	M	= Matthew
		L	= Luke

4 · Source Q

How much of Mark was made use of by Matthew and Luke is clear, but how much of Q it is impossible to know. All that can be checked is the material from Q used by Matthew and Luke together. It is quite possible that some Q material has been used only by Matthew, and some only by Luke, and therefore has been ascribed, not to Q, but to M and L separately.

Scholars have tried to reconstruct this document Q. They say that probably it was first written in Aramaic, and then was translated into Greek before Matthew and Luke made use of it. Possibly it was a handbook for Christian teachers. Q certainly contained a considerable amount of Jesus' teaching. Incidentally the teaching reveals Jesus' interest in nature, and the use that he made of illustrations from things in everyday life.

John the Baptist figures prominently in Q, but in every mention of him it is plain that he was only the forerunner of Jesus. As John had a considerable following (cf. Acts 19[1-7]), the first Christians had to emphasize his subordination to Jesus. Probably many regarded John as much more the traditional type of prophet and holy man. Probably also many people asked how Jesus could be the Messiah since he was so different from the sort expected. So Q, as well as insisting on the subordinate position of John, also tells, in the temptation stories, how Jesus rejected the popular role of Messiah.

A tragic feature of Q is Jesus' bitter disappointment over the lack of response from the Galilean cities, and his lament over Jerusalem. There is no indication that Q contained any of the Good Friday and Easter stories.

A few of the incidents taken from Q by Matthew and Luke are to be found also in Mark. Thus Mark and Q record the following: John the Baptist's preaching, the baptism of Jesus, sin against the Holy Spirit, the parable of The Mustard Seed, the mission of the disciples. But, since Mark's wording is rather different from theirs, it may be presumed that he got this information independently.

Main Contents of Q

The mission of John the Baptist, and the baptism of Jesus. Luke $3^{2-9,}$ $^{16-17, 21-22}$, Matthew $3^{7-12, 16-17}$

The temptations of Jesus. Luke 4^{1-13}, Matthew 4^{1-11}

John's message from prison, and Jesus' tribute to him. Luke 7^{18-35}, Matthew $11^{2-11, 16-19}$

Much of the Sermon on the Mount. Matthew Chapters 5–7

Sermon on the Plain and other teaching. Luke $6^{20-49,}$ $11^{2-4, 9-13}$, $12^{22-34,}$ $^{57-59}$, 13^{23-30}, 14^{34-35}, $16^{13, 16-18}$

Would-be disciples. Luke 9^{57-60}, Matthew 8^{19-22}

Missionary tour of the disciples. Luke $10^{2-16, 21-24}$, Matthew 9^{37-38}, $10^{10-13, 16}$, 11^{25-27}, 13^{16-17}

Sin against the Holy Spirit. Luke 11^{14-20}, Matthew 12^{22-27}

The centurion's servant. Luke 7^{1-10}, Matthew $8^{5-10, 13}$

The Mustard Seed and The Leaven. Luke 13^{18-21}, Matthew 13^{31-33}

Possibly The Great Supper and The Marriage Feast. Luke 14^{15-24}, Matthew 22^{1-10}

Possibly The Lost Sheep. Luke 15^{3-7}, Matthew 18^{12-14}

Possibly The Pounds and The Talents. Luke 19^{12-27}, Matthew 25^{14-30}

The lament for Jerusalem. Luke 13^{34-35}, Matthew 23^{37-39}

The coming of the Son of man. Luke $17^{22-27, 33-37}$, Matthew $24^{26-28,}$ $^{37-41}$.

5 · St. Mark's Gospel

We cannot be sure that the name associated with any of the Gospels is the name of its original author. It is Christian tradition that has associated the New Testament Gospels with particular people. The name of John Mark has been associated with the Gospel that now bears his name because:

(1) Some early Christian writers say that he was the author of a

Gospel that was closely connected with the apostle Peter. Thus, sometime between A.D. 100 and 150 Papias, Bishop of Hierapolis, wrote, 'Mark, having become Peter's interpreter, set down all that the apostle could remember of what Jesus had said and done.' Papias had personally talked with people who knew John Mark. Another writer, the bishop Irenaeus, wrote about A.D. 185, 'After their deaths (i.e. Peter and Paul) Mark, the disciple and interpreter of Peter, himself also handed down to us in writing the things which Peter had proclaimed.'

It is not possible to be certain whether Mark wrote while Peter was alive, or after he was martyred in the Neronian persecution. Perhaps Mark started his Gospel while Peter was alive, and then after his death completed it. It is thought likely that the Roman Christians specially asked Mark to write a life of Jesus, because, with Peter dead, they no longer had an eye-witness as a source of information. Thus the Gospel was written probably in Rome for Roman Christians, and about the year A.D. 65.

(2) Of all the New Testament Gospels this one gives the freshest account of Jesus' life. Most of it comes from the memory of someone who saw for himself the incidents recorded. We know, from the quotations above, that the eye-witness behind a Gospel that Mark wrote was Peter.

(3) Incidents involving Peter are numerous in this Gospel (1^{16}, 8^{29}, 9^5, 14^{66-72}, 16^7).

(4) The Gospel begins with Jesus' baptism. It was shortly after this that Peter met Jesus. The Gospel that Mark wrote, but which Peter directed, would be likely to begin at this point.

(5) Mark's Gospel alone makes mention of someone who could well have been Mark himself. This was the nameless young man who was in the Garden of Gethsemane when Jesus was arrested, and who apparently had nothing to do with the story.

6 · Characteristics of Mark's Gospel

(1) An important characteristic of this Gospel is its orderly arrangement. The ministry of Jesus is divided into two parts, the Galilean ministry and the journey to the Cross. The first part begins with the baptism of Jesus, and continues with a selection of miracles. The second part begins with Peter's confession at Caesarea Philippi and the transfiguration, and is followed by teaching on humility, marriage, divorce, and wealth. Chapters 11–16 contain a day to day account of Holy Week.

(2) Of all the Gospels Mark's is the most vivid and fresh in style. When passages such as 2^{1-12}, 4^{35-41}, 5^{1-20}, 5^{21-43} are compared with the

5

corresponding passages in Matthew and Luke the difference is noticeable.

(3) The aim of the author forms another characteristic. Many scholars regard this as the gradual unfolding of what is termed 'the Messianic Secret', that is, the fact that Jesus was the Messiah but did not claim to be so openly until the last week of his life. Thus the climax comes when the high priest asks Jesus, *Art thou the Christ?* and Jesus replies, *I am.*

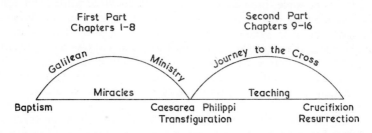

(4) Another characteristic arises from the fact that Mark was writing for Gentile Christians. Because of this he does not quote much from the Old Testament, and when he mentions Jewish customs he explains them (e.g. 2^{26}. cf. 7^2, 14^{12}, 15^{42}). Moreover, while he includes in his Gospel many of the Aramaic words that Jesus spoke, Mark translates them for the benefit of readers who are not Jews (e.g. 5^{41}. cf. 7^{11}, 7^{34}, 14^{36}, 15^{22}, 15^{34}).

(5) Mark shows quite fearlessly how slow were the disciples to understand Jesus, and how lacking they sometimes were in reverence towards him (e.g. 5^{31}).

7 · The Priority of Mark

(1) Point (5) of the previous section gives an indication of what scholars call the priority of Mark. Matthew and Luke modify his blunt portrayal of the Twelve, because at a later date the apostles had become revered figures in the Christian community, many of them having died as martyrs (cf. Mark 4^{38} with Luke 8^{24} and Matthew 8^{25}).

(2) Again Luke and Matthew modify phrases of Mark that might give rise to misunderstanding (cf. Mark 6^5 with Matthew 13^{58}, and Mark 10^{18} with Matthew 19^{17}, Luke 18^{19}).

(3) Most of Mark's Gospel is incorporated into Matthew and Luke; 95 per cent is in Matthew and 65 per cent is in Luke. This, and the fact that they use mainly the same order of events as he does, indicate that

Mark was already available as a source when Luke and Matthew came to write.

(4) If Luke and Matthew had existed first, and Mark had been able to use these Gospels as his sources, one would expect to find in Mark some mention of the birth stories, the Sermon on the Mount, and the resurrection appearances, as well as important parables such as The Prodigal Son and The Good Samaritan. Yet these are missing from Mark.

(5) Although Mark's is the shortest Gospel, his account of incidents is not only more vivid and fresh than that of the other Gospels, but also it contains more details. Furthermore, Luke consciously seeks to improve upon the literary style of Mark, and Matthew considerably abbreviates it. This sort of treatment seems to indicate a later development, and is very noticeable if the following accounts are compared:

The sick of the palsy.	Mark 2^{1-12},	Luke 5^{17-26},	Matthew 9^{1-8}
The storm at sea.	Mark 4^{35-41},	Luke 8^{22-25},	Matthew 8^{23-27}
Jairus' daughter.	Mark 5^{21-43},	Luke 8^{40-56},	Matthew 9^{18-26}

8 · St. Luke's Gospel

This Gospel was written by the same author as the Acts of the Apostles, for both documents are addressed to the same person (cf. Luke 1^3, Acts 1^1) and both agree in literary style. Since the Acts is commonly ascribed to Luke, the Gospel is so also.

Luke was an educated Gentile Christian. His home was probably Philippi or Troas. The New Testament speaks of him as a doctor of medicine (Colossians 4^{14}). Very ancient tradition says that he was also an artist, and that he painted a portrait of the Virgin Mary. Whether he was a painter or not, in point of literary style, Luke's is the most artistic Gospel.

Its possible date is calculated thus:

(1) Luke has used Mark, so his own Gospel must be later than about A.D. 65.

(2) In 21^{20} Luke describes the destruction of Jerusalem, which occurred in A.D. 70, as though it had actually taken place (although here it must be remembered that the writer, in anticipation of events, could as easily have drawn upon his imagination as upon his knowledge).

(3) By A.D. 96 Luke's Gospel was sufficiently well known for Clement of Rome to mention it in his own writings.

Therefore, allowing for the fact that all the Gospels were written and copied by hand, and so took time to get into circulation, a date of about A.D. 75–80, or possibly a little later, is likely.

7

There are two main theories about the arrangement of the Gospel:

(1) Luke took Mark's Gospel, and supplemented it with his own sources L and Q.

(2) He began with his own Gospel, consisting of sources L and Q, and inserted pieces from Mark. This is thought to be likely because Luke begins and ends with incidents from L, and because, if the material borrowed from Mark be removed, what remains is complete in itself.

The sources used by Luke were:

(1) 65 per cent of Mark.

(2) A source containing many of the incidents in Mark, which Luke prefers to Mark, or uses together with Mark.

(3) Part of document Q.

(4) A possible earlier edition of his own Gospel.

(5) His own particular source L, made up of (*a*) The birth stories (Chapters 1–2); (*b*) A source connected with Herod's court (8^3, 13^{31}); (*c*) The stories that Luke himself collected when staying with Philip the Evangelist (Acts 21^{8-10}); (*d*) Possibly some of document Q which, because it is not used also by Matthew, cannot be identified.

The sources that go to make up L were a mixture of oral tradition and written documents. The information in the birth stories may well have been obtained from Mary herself.

(A more detailed study of this subject may be found in *The Four Gospels* by R. H. Streeter.)

9 · Characteristics of Luke's Gospel

(1) Luke wrote his Gospel to give as full an account as possible of the grounds of the Faith to a high-ranking Gentile convert. The presentation of the life of Jesus is therefore designed to appeal to Gentile readers. Jesus is more than the Messiah of the Jews: he is the Saviour of the World. Thus:

(*a*) Luke omits all exclusively Jewish names, and puts in their place ones more widely used. For example, instead of rabbi and scribe, Luke writes master (or teacher) and lawyer. The Sea of Galilee is the Lake of Gennesaret.

(*b*) When giving dates, Luke uses the names of Roman emperors. Names of Jewish officials are mentioned last (2^1, 3^1).

(*c*) In giving a formal list of the ancestors of Jesus, Luke traces the genealogy back to Adam, regarded as the parent of the whole human race (cf. Matthew 1^{1-16}).

(d) Luke calls attention to Gentiles (e.g. in The Good Samaritan, The Ten Lepers, the Sermon at Nazareth, the Great Commission).

(2) Luke is interested not only in Gentiles, but also in the poor and the despised. Thus, Jesus was laid in a manger; poor shepherds were his first visitors; his mother gave turtledoves, the offering of the poor, at his presentation, and he, describing his own work, said, *To the poor the gospel is preached* (4^{18}, 7^{22}).

Two exclusive parables emphasize the importance of the poor (14^{16-24}, 16^{19-31}). A despised publican appears in 18^{9-14} and 19^{2-10}. A sinful woman figures in 7^{37-50}, and a penitent thief in 23^{39-43}. In Chapter 15 occur three parables all illustrating God's concern for the lost.

(3) In Luke's Gospel, as in the Acts, the importance of the Holy Spirit is stressed. He is the special possession of those most closely connected with Jesus' birth ($1^{15, 35, 41, 67}$, 2^{25-27}) and is often mentioned later (3^{22}, $4^{1, 18-21}$, 10^{21}, 11^{13}). The Gospel ends with the disciples waiting to *be clothed with power from on high*.

(4) Women, many of whom were possibly Luke's sources of information, are prominent. They include the widow of Nain, *Joanna the wife of Chuza, Herod's steward,* and the women on the way to Calvary.

(5) Joy, expressing itself in prayer, praise and thanksgiving, is a keynote of the Gospel (e.g. $2^{20, 28, 38}$, 7^{16}, 13^{13}, 17^{15}, 24^{52}). Outstanding in this respect are the four great songs, only to be found in this Gospel: The Magnificat (1^{46-55}), The Benedictus (1^{68-79}), The Gloria in Excelsis (2^{14}), The Nunc Dimittis (2^{29-32}).

(6) There is more mention in this Gospel than in any other of Jesus at prayer (3^{21}, 6^{12}, $9^{18, 29}$, 11^1, 22^{32}, $23^{34, 46}$). Three of the parables recorded only by Luke teach the need for persistence and humility in prayer: The Friend at Midnight (11^{5-13}), The Unjust Judge (18^{1-8}), The Pharisee and the Publican (18^{9-14}).

(7) In the Good Friday stories the note of tragedy is markedly absent as compared with the other Gospels: the coming victory of Jesus lightens the gloom of his death. Mention of the Agony in the Garden is absent from some early manuscripts.

10 · St. Matthew's Gospel

It is generally agreed that not all of Matthew's Gospel was written by Matthew the apostle. The author of the Gospel was not an eye-witness, as Matthew the apostle would have been. Mark's Gospel is the basis of it, and, where the author has used that source, the vivid and realistic details are missed out, leaving only the essential points.

Yet the name of Matthew the apostle has been associated with the Gospel since very early times. The early Christian historian Eusebius (A.D. 260–340) quotes the writings of three other Christian writers, Papias (A.D. 150), Irenaeus (A.D. 180), and Origen (A.D. 230), each of whom states that Matthew the apostle wrote a Gospel, or some sayings, in Hebrew or Aramaic.

Most scholars seem to be sure that Matthew's Gospel as we have it now was never in Hebrew before it appeared in Greek. Since our Matthew's Gospel contains most of Mark's Gospel, the Hebrew original must have contained either Mark's Gospel translated specially into Hebrew, or a Hebrew original of Mark. Mark's Gospel as it is now was written in Greek.

The Gospel ascribed to Matthew by the early writers already named may well have been either The Gospel of the Hebrews or The Gospel of the Nazarenes, both now lost. These were both written in Aramaic.

Another suggestion is that Matthew the apostle compiled a book of testimonies – a collection of texts from Jewish Scriptures which could be used by Christian teachers to prove that Jesus was the promised Messiah. The Gospel now bearing the name of Matthew contains frequent quotations from the Old Testament such as might have been taken from such a book.

A further possibility is that Matthew the apostle compiled a collection of Jesus' sayings, and that the author of Matthew (the Gospel) took from this collection the five groups of Jesus' teaching that are such a distinctive feature of the Gospel.

In general, Matthew's Gospel is written by an unknown Jewish Christian author, who used Mark, Q, and his own sources of information, which may well include genuine writings of the apostle. (For the sake of simplicity, both Gospel and author will be referred to in this book as 'Matthew'.)

The possible date of the Gospel depends upon several things:

(1) Matthew has used Mark's Gospel. His own must therefore be later than about A.D. 65.

(2) The Gospel seems to indicate that the fall of Jerusalem in A.D. 70 has already taken place. 23^{38} and 24^{15} appear to correspond closely with actual events; 22^7 is pointed too. But it appears from 24^3 that the writer is less interested in the fall of Jerusalem than in the Final Coming.

(3) The Gospel suggests that considerable time has passed between some events and their being written down, e.g. *until this day* in 27^8 and 28^{15}. It speaks of Pharisees and Sadducees together, two parties once quite distinct. After the Temple was destroyed the priestly Sadducean party ceased to exist. The Gospel is familiar with a developed system of Church discipline (18^{15-18}). In the first days of the Church, people were

baptized in the name of Jesus. In 28^{19} the Gospel quotes a form used later.

For these reasons the date usually given to the Gospel, as we have it, is A.D. 85–90.

11 · Characteristics of Matthew's Gospel

(1) The main characteristic is the aim of the author (or editor) to show Jewish-Christian readers that Jesus was the long-awaited Jewish Messiah. Thus:

(a) Matthew makes more use of the Jewish Scriptures than does any other Gospel writer, often introducing his frequent quotations with the formula *that it might be fulfilled.*

(b) He puts the title Son of David in places where it is not found elsewhere. For example, in Mark, blind Bartimaeus at Jericho is the first to use it. In Matthew, people healed much earlier do so (12^{23}), even foreigners (15^{22}). The Palm Sunday crowd does so (21^{9}).

(c) Matthew shows Jesus working only among his own people, the Jews. When he sent the Twelve on a missionary tour, he instructed them not to go to Gentiles and Samaritans (10$^{5-6}$). Mark tells of Jesus in Phoenician territory, and in a Gentile house (Mark 7^{24}). Matthew's account keeps Jesus within Jewish territory, and brings the Greek woman over the border to meet him (Matthew 15$^{21-24}$).

(2) Although Matthew was writing for Jewish Christians, his tone is often anti-Jewish. That was probably because Jewish converts encountered, more than did Gentile converts, the malice of Jewish attacks and tended to resent them. Scribes, Pharisees, and Jewish leaders receive in Matthew severe condemnation (3^{7}, 21^{43}). Chapter 23 contains a list of 'Woes' against scribes so bitter that many scholars think it to be an early Christian indictment rather than an actual statement by Jesus.

(3) Matthew's Gospel shows a marked interest in the End of All Things and in the Second Coming of Jesus. Mark 13, which deals with this difficult subject, is considerably expanded when used in Matthew 24. *There shall be weeping and gnashing of teeth* is a phrase often repeated. In the same way, Matthew frequently mentions *the end of the world*, which should more accurately be translated *the consummation of the age*, meaning that the present age would end or be completed when the day of judgement came, and Jesus' Second Coming occurred, for then a new age would begin.

(4) In order to make the miracles of Jesus more impressive, Matthew

makes his own adaptations of, and additions to, the stories that he takes from Mark. For example, he writes about two mad men healed in Gerasa, and two blind men at Jericho. The fruitless fig tree withers immediately (Matthew 21$^{19-20}$). Earthquakes are added to the accounts of the crucifixion and resurrection (Matthew 27$^{51-54}$, 28^{2}).

(5) What is called 'the ecclesiastical interest' of Matthew is another important characteristic. The author is writing as a member of a Christian community: his Gospel therefore reflects Christian Church life. But he writes also as a former member of the Jewish Church. Consequently the Gospel has a double Church interest. The word Church occurs only in this Gospel, and in two significant places, 16^{18}, 18^{17}.

(6) A further distinctive feature is the careful arrangement of subject matter. There is much more of Jesus' teaching in this Gospel than there is in Mark, and it is carefully arranged in five 'books' or groups, because, as Jews, Matthew's readers were accustomed to the five books of instruction that comprised the Law of Moses. It is likely that the Gospel was intended to be a sort of handbook of instruction for Jewish Christians. Much of |the teaching, especially in the first book, the Sermon on the Mount, is in verse, a method commonly employed by the rabbis to aid the memory of their pupils.

12 · Plan of Matthew's Gospel

Birth stories
Baptism and temptation

Book One: The Sermon on the Mount   Chapters 5–7
Three miracles of healing
Three miracles of power – over nature, spirits, and sin
Three miracles of restoration – of life, sight, and speech

Book Two: Teaching on Discipleship   Chapters 9^{36}–11^{1}
Jesus and John the Baptist
Criticism from Pharisees

Book Three: Parables of the Kingdom   Chapter 13$^{5-53}$
Death of John the Baptist
Feeding of five thousand
More opposition from Pharisees, Sadducees and scribes
Peter's confession of faith
The transfiguration

Book Four: Greatness and Forgiveness Chapters 18^1–19^1
   Questions about divorce and possessions
   The request of James and John
   Palm Sunday
   The day of questions
   Woes upon scribes and Pharisees

Book Five: The Messianic Judgement Chapters 24^4–26^1
   The Last Supper
   Crucifixion
   Resurrection

13 · Sources used in Matthew

(1) 95 per cent of Mark's Gospel
(2) Part of document Q
(3) The author's own particular source M made up of
   (*a*) A collection of sayings ⎫ possibly by
   (*b*) A collection of Christian proof-texts from ⎬ Matthew the
       the Jewish Scriptures ⎭ apostle
   (*c*) Possibly some of document Q which, because it is not used also
       by Luke, cannot be identified.

Important Incidents from Source M (that is, only to be found in Matthew's Gospel).

An angel appears to Joseph	Chapter 1
The wise men, flight into Egypt, and massacre of Bethlehem children	2
Jesus' reply to Peter's confession	16^{17-19}
The thirty pieces of silver, Judas' remorse, the silver returned, Judas' suicide	27^{3-10}
Pilate's wife's intervention	27^{19}
Pilate's hand-washing	27^{24-25}
The earthquake and apparitions at the crucifixion	27^{51-53}
The guard at the tomb	27^{62-66}
The earthquake at the resurrection	28^2
The bribing of the guards	28^{11-15}

13

Birth and Infancy

14 · Luke's Preface

Luke 1¹⁻⁴

Theophilus was probably a Roman official of high rank, and interested in Christianity. 'Theophilus' meaning Lover of God was possibly a cover name for him, because it might not have been wise to address a Christian document to him openly.

In referring to earlier attempts to write accounts of the Faith as it was received at the beginning from eye-witnesses, Luke was no doubt thinking in particular of Mark's Gospel, and of document Q, which were so useful to himself. He makes it clear that he had made careful study of the facts, so as to set them down accurately in order, and thereby confirm instructions previously given orally.

15 · Zacharias in the Temple

Luke 1⁵⁻²⁵

Herod, later known as Herod the Great, was King of Samaria, Galilee, Peraea, and Judaea. In religion he was Jewish, but, by keeping on friendly terms with the Emperor Augustus, he was able to maintain considerable local power, although Palestine was under Roman domination. He ruled as a typical oriental tyrant from 37 B.C. to 4 B.C. It was he who in 20 B.C. started the building of the third and last Jewish Temple.

Not only was Zacharias a priest, but his wife Elisabeth was of priestly descent, for Aaron her ancestor was the first Jewish high priest.

The Temple priests were divided into twenty-four courses or rotas. Each course was on duty twice a year, and for a week at a time. *The course of Abijah* was the name given to rota 8 (I Chronicles 24¹⁰). Burning incense in the inner sanctuary at the time of the morning and evening sacrifices, was a great privilege (the honour came only once in a lifetime), and lots were drawn to select the priest required.

Some scholars think that John may have belonged to the particular class of Jews called Nazarites, one of whose vows was to abstain from wine (cf. Numbers 6 and Judges 13). But the words in v. 15 may merely mean that John would lead a life of self-denial.

To *stand in the presence of God* indicated Gabriel's high rank, for in royal courts only officials of the highest rank were permitted to stand in the sovereign's presence. Gabriel, meaning 'man of God', is the name of an angel mentioned in Daniel 8[16], 9[21].

Zacharias' subsequent dumbness, a consequence not unusual after great shock or nervous strain, was naturally interpreted as being a punishment for his doubt, and a proof of the truth of Gabriel's words. The usual benediction (v. 22) was Numbers 6[24–26].

Elisabeth's words in v. 25 reflect the view that for a woman to be childless was a sign of God's displeasure.

16 · The Annunciation   Luke 1[26–38]

Luke is the only Gospel writer to mention Mary's home town. Joseph was a distant descendant of the royal house of David. Betrothal took place about a year before marriage, and was marked by solemn ceremony. Jesus was a late form of the name Joshua, and meant 'God is Salvation'.

Vv. 32–33 sum up the Jewish Messianic hope, the hope that one day God would restore the nation to the greatness and prosperity that it had known under King David. *Son of the Most High* implied a special and close relationship.

In Jewish writings *Son of God* was an expression used for a good man, for angels, for kings, or, collectively, for the whole nation. In Christian writings the title, when ascribed to Jesus, denoted a unique relationship with God.

Mary's response, *Behold the handmaid of the Lord. . . .* implies that she had had freedom to refuse her vocation.

17 · Mary's Visit to Elisabeth   Luke 1[39–56]

Mary had learned from the angel that her kinswoman (possibly aunt) also was expecting a child. The *city of Judah* was possibly Jutha, a city for priests not far from Hebron. The distance was about 75 miles from Nazareth. Elisabeth knew instinctively the reason for the visit, and greeted Mary as the mother of the Messiah (*My Lord*).

Mary's song of thanksgiving is known as the Magnificat, from its first word in Latin. It is based upon the Song of Hannah (I Samuel 2[1–10]) and is very similar, but the ideas contained in the Magnificat reflect also the Psalms and the prophets. The poetry of the Magnificat, as we have it, may to some extent be due to the way in which Luke had edited it, but the substance of it would belong to Mary herself. An alternative suggestion is that Mary made use of an existing Jewish hymn. (Some manuscripts attribute the Magnificat to Elisabeth.)

The time factor in v. 56 indicates that Mary stayed with Elisabeth until John was born.

18 · The Birth of John   Luke 1⁵⁶⁻⁸⁰

Eight days after the birth of Elisabeth's child, he was circumcised according to the Law (Leviticus 12³). Among the Jews circumcision was an outward sign of the solemn covenant that God had made with them. It seems that Zacharias was deaf as well as dumb: *they made signs* to him. The writing-tablet would consist of soft wax, in which marks were made with a metal stylus.

Zacharias' song is known as the Benedictus. Like Mary, he thanked God for his goodness to his people, and for remembering his promises made to Abraham. He rejoiced in the Jewish Messianic hope (expressed by the prophets), prophesied of his son, *Thou, child, shalt be called the prophet of the Most High*, and concluded with a hope that the Messianic Age was about to dawn.

The final form of the Benedictus, as with the Magnificat, is probably the work of Luke, who has edited it, but its contents belong to Zacharias, who, experienced as a priest and inspired by the Holy Spirit, could sum up in words from the Sacred Scriptures God's purpose for his people.

Since the discovery of the Dead Sea Scrolls some have suggested that John became a member of the austere monastic community once at Qumram, in the deserts near the Dead Sea. There is much in his character and message to make this a probability.

19 · The Birth of Jesus   Luke 2¹⁻²⁰, Matthew 2¹

It was Roman practice to hold a census or enrolment every fourteen years. Augustus Caesar was Rome's first emperor, and an able administrator. He promoted these enrolments as a means of obtaining statistics helpful for governing the empire. Quirinius, as far as can be ascertained, was twice governor of Syria, of which Roman province Judaea was a part, and each time that he was in office a census was held.

Luke says, *This was the first enrolment*. It is known that the second was in A.D. 6, so the first must have been begun about 8 B.C.

That all the world should be enrolled seems to indicate that the census took place in all parts of the empire, which in those days accounted for most of the known world. No trace of such a census has yet been found for any of the years in question. Possibly the enrolments under Quirinius were concerned only with Herod's kingdom. In that case *all the world* means all the Jewish world.

Roman enrolments did not involve a return to the place of birth. That this was done in Palestine was a Roman concession to the Jews, whose tribal system was still important.

There is no certainty about the year of Jesus' birth. It took place sometime between the possible beginning of the census, about 8 B.C., and the death of Herod the Great in 4 B.C. Matthew's stories of Jesus' childhood indicate that Jesus was about two years old when Herod died. So the year 6 B.C. is thought to be likely. Because of the delay caused by a Jewish census, Joseph's tribe might not have been involved until then.

That Jesus was probably born in a year 'before Christ' often puzzles people. Our system of dividing history into B.C. and A.D. was fixed in the sixth century, according to what was then thought to be the year of Jesus' birth. Since then more evidence has become available to help scholars in their calculations, and a date several years previous to that originally adopted is now suggested. Nevertheless it is easier to call this date B.C. than to alter all others.

Joseph, because he was a descendant of King David, had to go to Bethlehem, David's birthplace, six miles from Jerusalem. David had belonged to the tribe of Judah, so Judaea was the name given to the tribal territory. No city could have been more appropriate for the birth of Jesus. The prophet Micah (quoted in Matthew 2⁶) had written that Bethlehem would be the birthplace of the Messiah (Micah 5²). Since David had been born there, Micah must have thought it likely that the Son of David, that is the Messiah, would be born there also.

It is not certain that Mary was still only betrothed to Joseph. Some ancient manuscripts of Luke say that she was, but others describe her as 'his wife'. It is not certain either whether the census included the females of the population. If it did not, Mary probably chose to go with Joseph, rather than be left in Nazareth, where most likely she was the subject of gossip.

An Eastern inn, or khan, did not provide separate rooms for guests, only open recesses around an enclosed space. The stabling might well be more private. *Swaddling clothes* were long strips of linen, supposed to give strength to a baby's weak limbs. The manger, or feeding trough, was possibly a hollow in the floor. It is thought likely that the lambs cared for by the shepherds were specially reared for Temple sacrifices. In the Bible the expression *the glory of the Lord* commonly means the Shekinah or the presence of God.

20 · The Circumcision and Presentation   Luke 2²¹⁻⁴⁰

The regulations regarding circumcision and purification were fixed by Leviticus 12.

At the same time as a mother's purification ceremony, another ceremony, that of presentation, took place, if the son was the first-born male in a family. From very primitive times the first-born of humans and animals (and the first-fruits of crops) were regarded as God's special property. Sometimes they were offered as sacrifices. However, as religious beliefs developed, it became customary solemnly to present the first-born, and then to redeem him, or 'buy him back again', by making a substitute offering, eventually money, in his place (Exodus 13). *Their purification* in v. 22 seems intended to cover this complementary ceremony.

Simeon was probably a retired priest. V. 32 is reminiscent of Isaiah 49⁶, and v. 34 of the Fourth Servant Song in Isaiah 53. V. 36 means that Anna's married life lasted only seven years.

V. 39 gives no hint of Matthew's story of the Wise Men, but as this occurred later, and away from the stable, it would be possible for Joseph to return to Nazareth, and go to Bethlehem, his family home, a second time.

21 · The Nativity in Matthew   Matthew 1¹⁸⁻²⁵

Matthew begins his story at the point where, according to Luke, Mary had returned from her visit to Elisabeth.

Mary was only betrothed to Joseph, and so was still living with her parents. Even so a betrothal could not be ended without a divorce-letter being given to her in the presence of witnesses. Joseph did not want any publicity for Mary, and so contemplated a private annulment, if she were willing, her parents being the witnesses required. The alternative was a public affair in the presence of three rabbis.

Why did Joseph consider ending his betrothal to Mary? Being a *righteous man*, did he believe her to be guilty of immoral conduct, and therefore not a wife fit for him, or, because he was a righteous man, did he believe her story, and so feel that, because she belonged to God, she was too good for him? The second reason is more likely, for, had Joseph believed Mary guilty, the matter would not have weighed so heavily upon his mind. The Greek of 'when he thought on these things' (in v. 20) may be translated 'while he was pondering upon these things'.

The point of v. 21 is that the name Jesus is a Greek form of the Hebrew name Jeshua, or Joshua, and means 'God is Salvation'.

V. 23 is the first of Matthew's many quotations from the Jewish Scriptures. It is taken from Isaiah 7^{14}. The context there shows that a young woman bearing a son with the name Immanuel (meaning 'God with us') was to be a special sign from God to King Ahaz of Judah, then extremely anxious about the military intentions of his neighbours the Kings of Syria and Ephraim. The child would eat only curds and wild honey, because the land would be out of cultivation, but even before he was old enough to know the difference between good and evil (that is, while he was still an infant) the enemies of Ahaz would be overthrown.

The Hebrew of Isaiah, and the Greek of Matthew, which are translated *virgin*, do not necessarily imply a virgin in the biological sense, but simply mean a young woman of marriageable age.

It is easy to see why Matthew, writing for Jewish Christians, thought the quotation important. It told of a child in the past who signified that God was with his people. He himself was writing about a Child who represented that truth even more so.

22 · The Wise Men Matthew 2$^{1-12}$

The visit of the wise men took place some time after the presentation in the Temple recorded by Luke. This is indicated by the words *house* and *young child* in v. 11, and the time factor in v. 16.

The star in v. 2 is a subject of much interest. Between the years 1603 and 1606 a most unusual phenomenon was observed by the astronomer Kepler. A conjunction of the planets Saturn and Jupiter occurred in the Zodiacal sign of Pisces (Fishes). A few months later the planet Mars joined them. A few months later still what seemed to be a new and very bright star appeared between Mars and Saturn. After shining for a year it disappeared.

This sort of conjunction of planets happens only once in about eight hundred years. Kepler, by calculations, discovered that this had been visible three times over in the year 7 B.C. Such conjunction was more than enough to cause the phenomenon of an exceptionally bright star just before the birth of Jesus, and incidentally one particularly visible in and around Jerusalem. The appearance of such a star would certainly suggest that a special event either had taken place or was about to do so.

At this time there was widespread expectation among the peoples of the East that a world deliverer would appear in the West. Many people believed that the appearance of a star heralded the coming of a great person. A star was connected with the births of Alexander the Great and of Augustus, the Emperor at the time of Jesus' birth. The Jews believed in the importance of stars as did people around them. A Jewish story tells how some astrologers dining with Terah observed a special star on the night when Abraham was born. The prophecy of Balaam (Numbers 24^{17}) prompted a Jewish rebel, who fancied himself as a Messiah, to call himself Bar-cochab (Son of a Star) when he led the final Jewish revolt against the Romans in A.D. 131.

It would be natural therefore for the wise men, being learned men acquainted with the literature of their time, including the Jewish Scriptures, to assume that a star indicated the coming of the Jewish Messiah, and also for them to carry with them as gifts representative products of their countries.

The quotation in v. 6 is from Micah 5^2. *The princes of Judah* mean either the principal cities, or the places thought of as represented by their local rulers (as often in Shakespeare).

It seems clear that the movement, or apparent movement, of the star is regarded in v. 9 as miraculous, but the statement that *the star went before them* need mean no more than that the star continued to be ahead of them as they travelled in its direction, and was at its zenith over Bethlehem.

In Christian thought, the gold in v. 11 was symbolic of the kingship of Jesus, frankincense (associated with worship) acknowledged him as divine, and myrrh (used both as a healing ointment and for anointing the dead) indicated his suffering and death. The number and richness of the gifts have suggested that the givers were three kings (with the traditional names of Caspar, Melchior, and Balthazzar). Isaiah 60^3 and Psalm 72$^{10-11}$ have been regarded as foreshadowing that they were Gentile kings. In art one is usually depicted dark-skinned.

A different interpretation is occasionally given, based on the Greek word translated as wise men – Magi. The name Magi was given to oriental priest-scholars of the Zoroastrian religion of Persia, and also to those who practised astrology and magic arts (magicians). Astrology is a very ancient, and not necessarily insincere study, but it has been argued that 'wise men' approximated to 'wise women' in witchcraft, and that these were wise men who, after first seeking employment at Herod's court, travelled hopefully to Bethlehem, and then felt moved to abandon their profession, and give up their money and equipment.

It would seem that this interpretation of Matthew's story demands rather more credence than the story itself. Matthew's story is possibly idealized, but the main truth of it is not unreasonable.

23 · The Escape to Egypt   Matthew 2¹³⁻²³

In Egypt there lived quite a flourishing Jewish community, and among these Joseph would settle.

There is no contemporary record of the slaughter of the children of Bethlehem, but such an action on Herod's part is quite in keeping with his character. Possibly, as compared with his other crimes, the murder of perhaps two dozen babies was too insignificant to deserve recording.

In vv. 17 and 18 Matthew quotes as appropriate Jeremiah 31¹⁵. Rachel was the favourite wife of Jacob, and her tomb was not far from Bethlehem. When Jeremiah wrote he was describing the sad sight of hundreds of Jews being taken to captivity in Babylon, after Jerusalem had been captured by King Nebuchadnezzar. On their way to exile the captives passed by the tomb of Rachel, their great ancestress. Jeremiah felt that such a tragic sight was enough to make her weep in her grave.

In v. 15 Matthew recalls as appropriate Hosea 11¹. Hosea was writing about the way in which God had called the Hebrews (referred to collectively as *my son*) from captivity in Egypt in the time of Moses. Very much in the mind of Matthew, as he wrote of these happenings in the early life of Jesus, was the story of the early life of Moses, the first great deliverer of the Jewish people, himself saved from a massacre ordered by a cruel king (Exodus 1²²).

In his will Herod had bequeathed his kingdom to his three sons, Archelaus, Antipas, and Philip. Mary and Joseph intended to return to Bethlehem. It was Joseph's family town, and Jesus' birthplace. Perhaps also there would still be gossip about them in Nazareth. When, however, they realized that Judaea was now ruled by Archelaus, who could be as cruel as his father had been, they decided that Nazareth, Mary's town, in the territory of Antipas, would be safer. Besides Bethlehem would still contain people who remembered the disaster that this family had brought upon them.

Thus Jesus came to spend most of his early life in the obscurity of Nazareth, fulfilling this time an untraceable prophecy, *He should be called a Nazarene.*

24 · Twelve Years Old   Luke 2⁴⁰⁻⁵²

Male Jews were commanded to go to the Temple at least three times a year, for the feasts of Passover, Pentecost, and Tabernacles (Exodus 23¹⁴⁻¹⁷). Many Jews who lived at great distances from Jerusalem were unable to go so often, and attended only once a year. Joseph was in the habit of going to Jerusalem, 80 miles away from Nazareth, for the

Passover celebrations. Mary went with him, although there was not the same obligation for her.

Twelve is an important age for a Jewish boy, for it marks the beginning of his being grown-up and assuming full adult responsibility, especially in matters of Jewish Law. During the year between his twelfth and thirteenth birthday he receives a course of special instruction from a rabbi. Then at the age of thirteen a boy reads the Law for the first time in the synagogue, and becomes 'a Son of the Law', a fully adult member of the community, entitled to wear the tallith (prayer shawl) and tephillin (phylacteries, small leather boxes containing the Shema (Deuteronomy 6⁴⁻⁵) and other Bible passages, one worn on the head and one on the left arm, as a reminder that God's Law must always be in the mind and governing one's actions).

Jesus had been to the Temple before, but he would not remember that occasion. He probably realized that he was lost, and sensibly stayed in one place, the obvious one, until he was found.

Christians, like Mary, have meditated much upon Jesus' first recorded words. Was Jesus in v. 49 just expressing surprise that Mary and Joseph had not thought of looking for him in the Temple first of all? It was not an unheard of thing for Jews to speak of God as *Father*, and a devout Jew might call the Temple *my Father's house*. Or had the words a deeper significance?

It is not possible to know how or when Jesus became conscious of a special relationship with God. The Gospels indicate that his physical and mental advancement were normal enough, so the spiritual realization that God was his Father in a unique way may also have been a gradual process. Possibly therefore a dawning consciousness of this unique relationship, and of a unique mission, is reflected in the words.

Nor is it known when Mary first told Jesus about the unusual circumstances of his birth. At the age of twelve, and before this visit to Jerusalem, would have been an appropriate time. But perhaps Jesus' words in the Temple surprised Mary because he had not been told yet, and it was obviously time that he should be.

25 · The Genealogies Luke 3²³⁻³⁸, Matthew 1¹⁻¹⁷

Both these 'family trees' of Jesus trace his ancestry through Joseph and not Mary, because it was the male descent that Jews regarded as important. When Joseph married Mary his pedigree became hers, and her son was thus legally his heir.

Neither of the genealogies is meant to give an accurate list of Jesus' ancestors. The names in the two lists agree only from Abraham to David. The lists are representative only. Their purpose was to show that Jesus was a descendent of King David, and a descendant of Abraham to whom God made the promise, *in thee shall all the families of the earth be blessed* (Genesis 12³).

Matthew's genealogy ends with Abraham, the father of the Jews, because Matthew was writing his Gospel especially for Jewish Christians. Luke, writing for Gentiles, traces the ancestry of Jesus back to Adam, regarded as the father of all mankind.

26 · The Birth Stories of Jesus

Some scholars regard the birth stories as little more than a collection of myths and legends, and for these reasons:

(1) Many legends have grown up around the great heroes of ancient history, and it is suggested that Luke and Matthew show the early Christians giving the same treatment to Jesus, using ingredients from other sources to compile suitable stories for him. Even the Old Testament could supply material: e.g. Three angels told Abraham that his aged wife would have a son (Genesis 18¹⁻¹⁵). An angel visited Samson's mother to announce his birth (Judges 13). Hannah sang a song of thanksgiving for the birth of Samuel (I Samuel 2¹⁻¹⁰).

(2) Stars announcing the births of famous people (e.g. Abraham, Alexander the Great, and Augustus) are by no means uncommon in literature. In A.D. 66 some Parthians came to pay homage to the Emperor Nero, believing him to be the god Mithras in human form. In Isaiah 60⁶ gold and incense are mentioned as offerings. The story of the escape of Jesus to Egypt, and the slaughter of the children at Bethlehem, is faintly reminiscent of the early life of Moses.

(3) The birth stories contain very many supernatural happenings, and in particular angels and warnings in dreams.

(4) There are the questions why Luke does not mention the Magi, and why Matthew, in the story of the return from Egypt, mentions Nazareth as though it were new to Mary and Joseph. Why is the birth of Jesus but little referred to anywhere afterwards?

These considerations lead such scholars to regard the stories of the shepherds and wise men as true only symbolically. In this view, the shepherds represent Jesus' own people the Jews, and the wise men represent the Gentile world, and so between them they symbolize the homage of all mankind. Furthermore, though the shepherds were poor and simple, and the wise men rich and learned, all were equally led to the infant Jesus.

23

Against all this, there is plenty of good reason for supposing that the main contents of the birth stories are based upon fact. Thus:

(1) Myths and legends grow up around the name of an important person who lived in a distant past. So far as the first Christians were concerned Jesus did not live in a distant past. Many of them had known him personally, and Mary his mother, an obvious source of information, was herself a member of the early Christian community (Acts 1^{14}).

(2) Even myths and legends are based upon an element of truth. So may the birth stories be.

(3) The simplicity and dignity of the stories are points in their favour. In the mention of supernatural happenings the writers are very restrained, and give no hint of striving to impress.

(4) The underlying historical facts of the birth stories are reasonably certain. There probably was a Roman census at the time of Jesus' birth; Augustus was the Emperor; Herod the Great was the Jewish king; Quirinius was ruling in Syria; Jews insisted upon being enrolled at their birth-places; Mary would present her firstborn in the Temple; there very likely was a bright star; people of the East were expecting a deliverer in the West; gold, frankincense, and myrrh, were products of Eastern lands; Herod was quite capable of a massacre; Egypt had a considerable Jewish colony.

(5) As the details of the adult life of Jesus given in the Synoptic Gospels are commonly regarded as mainly historical, it is but reasonable to accept the birth stories in the same way, and, contrariwise, unreasonable not to do so.

(6) The reason why no special mention of the birth stories is made in the preaching of the first Christians, or in any of the Epistles, may well be that the resurrection, being more recent, and of more immediate importance, claimed more attention.

27 · The Virgin Birth

The widespread and very ancient Christian belief that Jesus was born of a human mother, without the agency of a human father, is based mainly upon the following passages from the Gospels:

(a) Mary said unto the angel, How shall this be, seeing I know not a man? And the angel answered and said unto her, The Holy Ghost shall come upon thee, and the power of the Most High shall overshadow thee: wherefore also that which is to be born shall be called holy, the Son of God (Luke 1$^{34, 35}$).

(b) Jesus himself, when he began to teach, was about thirty years of age, being the son (as was supposed) of Joseph (Luke 3²³).

(c) Joseph the husband of Mary, of whom was born Jesus, who is called Christ (Matthew 1¹⁶).

(d) When his mother Mary had been betrothed to Joseph, before they came together she was found with child of the Holy Ghost (Matthew 1¹⁸).

(e) Fear not to take unto thee Mary thy wife: for that which is conceived in her is of the Holy Ghost (Matthew 1²⁰).

(f) And took unto him his wife; and knew her not till she had brought forth a son (Matthew 1²⁵).

Some scholars question the virgin birth (strictly speaking, the virgin conception) on the following grounds:

(1) The relevant passages in the Gospels could have been inserted into Luke and Matthew by someone who wanted to imply a virgin birth for Jesus.

(2) Jesus is often referred to in the Gospels as being the son of Joseph (John 1⁴⁵), and Mary and Joseph are spoken of as *his parents* (Luke 2⁴¹, ⁴³). In the story of the presentation in the Temple, Luke says, *And when the days of their purification . . . were fulfilled* (2²²). Some suggest that here *their* refers to Joseph and Mary, as being Jesus' parents. (This can hardly be so, for it was the mother only who needed purification. More likely *their* means here Mary and Jesus, her purification and his presentation having made for them a double ceremony.)

(3) Apart from the infancy stories there are no other definite mentions of the virgin birth in the New Testament.

(4) The infancy stories have certain features in common with the myths and legends of more ancient religions.

(5) Such a thing as a virgin birth would be impossible physically.

As against these objections the following points need to be considered (the numbering corresponds to the objections):

(i) In all the ancient manuscripts of the Gospels the first five quotations listed above are to be found. The second part of quotation *(f)* is missing in some manuscripts. This fact is strong evidence that the quotations were written by the authors of the Gospels themselves, and not added later. Scholars agree that the most important quotation of all (the first) was written by Luke, and not by someone imitating Luke.

(ii) That Jesus is sometimes described as the son of Joseph is no evidence against the virgin birth. Legally Joseph was his father, and the general public, knowing nothing of the birth of Jesus, would naturally regard him as the son of Joseph, and Mary and Joseph as his parents. The descriptions are cast in the normal language of society, as adoptive parents in our day are usually addressed by their adopted children as Father and Mother.

(iii) The silence of the rest of the New Testament may be accounted for by consideration for the Virgin Mary, a desire to avoid misunderstanding with Gentiles, and mockery from the scornful, and by preoccupation with the main theme of Christian preaching – Jesus and the resurrection. As for Mark's Gospel, the nativity was outside its plan. Immediately following the period when the New Testament was written, however, at the turn of the same century, we have Ignatius, the famous martyr-bishop of Antioch, making clear mention of the virgin birth in letters that he wrote not long before his death.

(iv) The so-called virgin birth legends come from primitive religions in which man's desire for fertility among crops, flocks, and herds, led people to worship male and female deities. These gods and goddesses had children by one another, and sometimes the gods mated with mortal women. The children thus born were the result not of virgin births, but, as we may say, of mixed marriages between immortals and mortals. There is nothing so crude as this in the story of Jesus' virgin birth. The miracle of his conception is ascribed to the power of the Holy Spirit.

Furthermore, the myths and legends come from the time when people believed in gods and goddesses, but the Jews had long passed beyond that stage of religion. Since the first Christians were Jews, for them to invent a virgin birth for their master, or accept such an idea from some other source, would be a return to the primitive. For them to expect the idea to be believed would be equally unlikely.

Christians see in these early stories a remarkable foreshadowing of the life of Jesus, who fulfils all religious speculation and groping after truth down the centuries.

(v) The main reason for accepting the virgin birth as part of the historical content of the infancy stories lies more in the realm of theology than of scripture. The basic Christian belief is that God entered the world to live the life of a human being. This is called the Incarnation, and, if one can accept it as a fact, most of the New Testament miracles, including the virgin birth and the resurrection, become reasorable. If the supreme wonder could occur, all else in the Gospels becomes possible and likely.

In this connection, in so far as the New Testament scriptures show that the early Christians believed in the divinity of Jesus, the scriptures may be said to support, at least indirectly, belief in the virgin birth.

Beginning of the Ministry

28 · The Ministry of John the Baptist Mark 1^{1-8}. Luke 3^{1-18}.
Matthew 3^{1-12}

Mark begins by quoting Malachi 3^1 and Isaiah 40^3. The second passage
was written during the exile in Babylon, by an unknown prophet who
was hoping that soon the exiles would return to Jerusalem, led by God
along a smooth and level highway, stretching over the desert. Both
passages seemed to Mark appropriate to the work of John the Baptist.

Jews believed that before the Messiah came a prophet would herald
his coming. Some even thought that Elijah would come again to do this.
Mark, however, wished to show that John the Baptist was the herald-
prophet. While not in fact Elijah, John was very similar. Like Elijah he
lived hard, appeared suddenly, spoke boldly, rebuked a king, an-
tagonized a queen, endangered his own life. John's diet was either locust
insects or locust beans, which grew wild. He was the first great prophet
to appear for 400 years.

Baptism was common among Jews as a ritual washing. One such
occasion for it was the reception of proselytes (converts). Unlike
Christian Baptism, ritual washings were often repeated, as acts of
piety. John related his baptism to a remission of sins.

LUKE. Many of John's hearers thought that the divine judgement that
he foretold would affect only Gentiles, but John, like the Old Testament
prophets before him, told them that being Jews (Abraham's children)
would not save them. As God's chosen people their responsibility was
much greater than that of Gentiles. The *wrath to come* meant the Day
of the Lord foretold by the prophets (e.g. Amos 5^{18}, Malachi 4^5). Note
John's practical advice to people to show the reality of their repentance.
The fan in Luke 3^{17} was a spade-shaped farm implement used on a
threshing floor for separating chaff from corn.

MATTHEW. Instead of the multitude, as in Luke 3^7, Matthew, charac-
teristically, has *Pharisees and Sadducees*.

27

29 · Jesus Baptized by John
Mark 1⁹⁻¹¹. Luke 3²¹⁻²³. Matthew 3¹³⁻¹⁷

Jesus' baptism was an act of dedication for his future work, of identification with humanity, of personal humility, and of approval of John's work.

The voice from heaven recalled Psalm 2⁷ and Isaiah 42¹, the first of the Songs of the Suffering Servant. How sure Jesus was before his baptism that he was the Messiah is not known, but this voice convinced him of his call. The dove-like coming of the Spirit (also mentioned in Isaiah 42¹) gave a clue to the peaceful sort of Messiah that he was to be.

Mark describes what happened from the point of view of Jesus. *He saw the heavens rent asunder, and the Spirit as a dove descending.* Luke says, *the heaven was opened, and the Holy Ghost descended in a bodily form, as a dove.* Matthew tends to follow Mark, *The heavens were opened unto him, and he saw the Spirit of God descending as a dove.* From this it seems to be an open question whether there was an actual dove, or Jesus received the Spirit as quietly and peacefully as a dove might alight.

On the other hand Mark 1¹¹, and the corresponding verses in Luke and Matthew, indicate that the voice was audible generally.

Notice Mark's favourite use (and probably Peter's) of *straightway* in vv. 10 and 12.

30 · The Temptations
Mark 1¹²⁻¹³. Luke 4¹⁻¹⁵. Matthew 4¹⁻¹¹

Jesus' growing awareness of himself as the Messiah had been confirmed by the voice and the Spirit at his baptism. In the wilderness afterwards he reflected upon that experience, and decided how to proceed next. In doing so he had to resist certain temptations.

The temptations are inevitably pervaded with mystery. In what order they affected Jesus we do not know. Probably they shaped and re-shaped themselves as the days passed by. Most likely what we have is a description of the temptations in their final and most acute form. The information must have come originally from Jesus himself.

(1) According to the Gospels Jesus was tempted first in regard to his miraculous powers. So far they had not been used. His hunger provided circumstances in which to test them, and with them his Messiahship. *If thou art the Son of God,* queried the devil. The temptation was resisted. Jesus did not intend to use his miraculous powers on his own behalf.

Bound up with his decision was one not to supply the material needs of people in isolation from their spiritual needs, not to found, as it were, a sort of earthly welfare state. A great moral principle was involved. *Man shall not live by bread alone* . . . (Deuteronomy 8³).

(2) Another temptation concerned the sort of Messiah that Jesus would be. Little noticed in the Old Testament, in the writings of Second Isaiah, were what are known as the Songs of the Suffering Servant, or the Servant Songs. These spoke of a Messiah who would be the suffering servant of God. God's Spirit would be upon him. He would suffer innocently for the sins of others, but eventually would triumph (Isaiah 42¹⁻², 49¹⁻⁶, 50⁴⁻⁹, and especially 52¹³–53¹²). This was the way to Messiahship that Jesus chose.

In the wilderness, however, came the temptation to adopt the devil's methods, and seek by military conquest to become a benevolent dictator. The idea was doubly attractive. Jews commonly believed that the Messiah would reclaim for God those parts of the world over which the devil was supposed to hold power, especially the heathen world; a military Messiah was the sort that most people expected. The distant views that the wilderness afforded gave stimulus to the imagination. Jesus resisted the temptation and quoted Deuteronomy 6¹³ to the effect that whole-hearted service of God excluded any sort of alliance with the devil.

(3) There was also a temptation for Jesus to begin his career in some spectacular way. His mind strayed away from the wilderness to a pinnacle, or wing, of the Temple, and the crowds thronging the courts below. The Temple was thought to be the place where the Messiah would most likely first appear. A leap from the summit would command attention and win respect. It would disclose, moreover, whether God was indeed behind him. The devil persuasively quoted Scripture (Psalm 91¹¹, ¹²), but Jesus, quoting a third time from Deuteronomy (6¹⁶), retorted that it was wrong to think of putting God to any test.

The words *for a season* in Luke 4¹³ gain point when one thinks of the subsequent temptations in Gethsemane and Calvary.

This is the order of the temptations in Luke. Matthew reverses the order of the last two, and slightly varies the dialogue between Jesus and the devil. Mark's only detail is the one about the angels. *Forty days* was a Jewish expression symbolic of a long time, but fasting as long is not unknown in modern times.

31 · The Imprisonment of John Luke 3¹⁸⁻²⁰

Herod the Tetrarch (or ruler over a fourth part of a larger territory) was Herod Antipas, a son of King Herod the Great (notorious for his massacre of the infants at Bethlehem).

The cause of the reproof in v. 19 is given in greater detail in Mark 6^{14-19}, and dealt with in Section 84.

32 · The Call of the First Disciples
Mark 1^{14-20}. Luke 5^{1-11}. Matthew 4^{12-22}

It is very likely that Jesus had made the acquaintance of these men before, and that they had agreed to join him when the time came (cf. John 1^{35-42}). It is not, however, a thing unheard of in the East for people suddenly to follow an unknown 'holy man'.

LUKE. In Luke the call is preceded by an account of Jesus preaching from one of the boats and a miracle. Andrew is not mentioned, but Peter is prominent. This is probably because, by the time the Gospel was written, Peter had become the leading member of the Church.

MATTHEW. In addition to Mark's account, Matthew adds a quotation in vv. 15 and 16 from Isaiah $9^{1, 2}$. Like numerous others it probably came from a collection of texts from the Old Testament used by Christian teachers.

33 · The Healing of a Demoniac
Mark 1^{21-28}. Luke 4^{31-37}

According to Jewish custom any man could be invited by the ruler of a synagogue to preach a sermon, especially if he were a distinguished visitor. People found Jesus' teaching a refreshing change from the formal expositions and interpretations of the Law, of which sermons by scribes consisted. Their authority was derived from the Law and the opinions of famous rabbis. The authority of Jesus was personal and direct.

The authority of Jesus was shown also in his actions: the Spirit World recognized his authority and obeyed him. Jews believed that mental illness was caused by demon possession. Mark is particularly interested in miracles of exorcism (i.e. the casting out of evil spirits). For him the evil spirits recognized Jesus as the Messiah even if human beings did not.

LUKE. Luke closely follows Mark.

34 · The Healing of Peter's Mother-in-Law

Mark 1²⁹⁻³⁴.
Luke 4³⁸⁻⁴¹.
Matthew 8¹⁴⁻¹⁷

The Jewish Sabbath is reckoned from sunset to sunset. Thus sick people were brought to Jesus *at even*, as soon as the Sabbath was over. Mark makes separate mention of demoniacs, because he is anxious to show that the spirits knew who Jesus was. *Took her by the hand* strengthens the view that Mark is reporting the recollections of an eye-witness (Peter).

LUKE. Luke's account is almost the same as Mark's, but he does not mention this detail.

MATTHEW. Matthew's account is shorter than either Mark's or Luke's. He does not mention that it was the Sabbath day, and, whereas Mark says that *all* the sick and demon-possessed were brought to Jesus and that he healed *many*, Matthew says that *many* were brought and *all were healed*. This was meant to correct any impression that Jesus was unable to heal all who came to him.

Matthew saw the healing work of Jesus as a fulfilment of the words of the prophet in the fourth of the Songs of the Suffering Servant (Isaiah 53⁴).

35 · Jesus at Prayer

Mark 1³⁵⁻³⁹. Luke 4⁴²⁻⁴⁴

During the temptations in the wilderness Jesus had resolved not to take personal advantage of his miraculous powers, nor to use them at any time apart from his teaching. So here he refuses to return to Capernaum, where people were looking for more miracles, and goes elsewhere to give priority to simple preaching.

LUKE. Luke's account is similar to that of Mark, except that Luke does not say that Jesus was at prayer, but rather that he was trying to slip away from Capernaum unobserved.

36 · Healing a Leper

Mark 1⁴⁰⁻⁴⁵. Luke 5¹²⁻¹⁶, Matthew 8¹⁻⁴

This miracle is narrated by Mark to show the power of Jesus over disease. Leprosy was a dreaded disease which caused the flesh to wither away. A leper was not allowed to mix with other people, or to come near their towns and houses. If anyone approached, a leper had to give a warning cry. If a person did recover from leprosy (and this was a term

31

sometimes used for other skin ailments) the Law required him to come before a priest and offer sacrifice before he was pronounced 'clean' (Leviticus 14$^{1-32}$).

Healing by touch was Jesus' usual method, but by touching a leper, in disregard of the ritual Law, Jesus made himself ceremonially 'unclean'. The command *See thou say nothing* was given because Jesus did not wish by his miracles to attract sightseers. Most miracles of healing were followed by this command. The leper disobeyed the command, and as a result Jesus had to remain in the open country. The command *Show thyself to the priest* shows Jesus' loyalty to the Law of Moses, even though he had disregarded the ritual law.

LUKE. Luke closely follows Mark, but places the miracle after the call of Peter.

MATTHEW. Matthew places the incident after the Sermon on the Mount. His account is a rather more abbreviated form of Mark.

37 · The Sick of the Palsy

Mark 2$^{1-12}$. Luke 5$^{17-26}$. Matthew 9$^{1-8}$

Jesus healed the man's body both to prove that he could do things easy to say but hard to check, and, because according to Jewish belief sin caused sickness, to show that the man's sins were indeed forgiven. Mark tells the story to show how the incident revealed the divinity of Jesus. It is the first time in Mark's Gospel that Jesus called himself *Son of Man*.

This is the only miracle associated with forgiveness.

LUKE. Luke follows Mark.

MATTHEW. Matthew omits Jesus' question about *which is easier* but adds the words *which had given such power unto men*. The words may imply that Jesus had used the term *Son of man* only to mean men in general (Psalm 8^4), and was not making an exclusive claim for himself. More likely they reflect the view of the early Christian community from which the Gospel comes that God had given such power to certain specific representatives of Jesus.

38 · The Call of Matthew

Mark 2$^{13-17}$. Luke 5$^{27-32}$. Matthew 9$^{9-13}$

Publicans were public officials who collected taxes for the Romans. No self-respecting Jew would do this work, so less honest types undertook the task, and exacted and embezzled all that they could. Publicans were despised and hated by all patriotic Jews.

Sinners were people who did not keep the Law of Moses in all its details. They mixed with Gentiles, as did the publicans, and so made themselves 'unclean'. Strict Jews believed that salvation lay in keeping the Law completely. Those who did not so keep it were considered outcasts, and no professedly holy man would associate with them.

This story shows the beginning of opposition to Jesus by Jewish officials because he mixed with and befriended these classes.

It is Matthew 9^9 that identifies the Levi of Mark 2^{14} and Luke 5^{27} with Matthew. *His house* in Mark 2^{15} could mean either Levi's or Jesus'. Luke 5^{29} makes it Levi's.

LUKE. Luke follows Mark, except that here the scribes and Pharisees ask why the disciples eat with publicans and sinners. Luke also adds *to repentance* to *call the righteous but sinners*.

MATTHEW. Here Levi is called Matthew, and a quotation from Hosea 6^6 is added in v. 13 to show the principle upon which Jesus worked.

39 · A Question about Fasting   Mark 2^{18-22}. Luke 5^{33-39}.   Matthew 9^{14-17}

Disciples of John the Baptist and of the Pharisees regularly fasted; the disciples of Jesus did not. In justification Jesus compared himself and his companions to a wedding party, and a wedding was no time for fasting.

The Jews had long thought of God's covenant with them as a marriage contract in which he was the bridegroom and they were the bride (Jeremiah 3^{14}, Hosea 2^{19}), and of the Messianic Kingdom as a banquet in which bridegroom and bride would rejoice together. Possibly Jesus was thinking of himself, the Messiah of God, as now presiding at that wedding feast, and shortly to be taken from it.

Some scholars suggest that this question arose after John's death, and that that was why his disciples were fasting: their 'bridegroom' had been taken away. But would that be of any interest to the Pharisees? It is more probable that the Pharisees mentioned John when criticizing Jesus because John, an ascetic man likely to encourage fasting, was setting a different example, and Jesus claimed to be in sympathy with John.

In speaking of the bridegroom as being *taken away* Jesus may already have had a premonition about his future.

In v. 21 Jesus mentions that no one mends a hole in an old garment with a piece of new undressed cloth, because the patch would shrink, and the tear would be worse than before. In v. 22 he refers to the custom of putting new wine into fresh wineskins. As the wine fermented the latter would easily stretch. To put new wine into old skins would be unsafe, because the leather would already have been stretched, and under the new strain would burst.

This was Jesus' way of saying that it is difficult to combine the new with the old. His teaching was the new patch and the new wine. The Jewish religion was the old garment and the old wineskin. There was bound to be tension when the two were brought together. Already opposition towards Jesus, and his new teaching, was growing. Eventually his Church would break away from the limits of Judaism and overflow among the Gentiles.

LUKE. Luke follows Mark, but rather spoils the saying, for nobody would think of mending an old coat by taking a patch from a new one.

MATTHEW. Matthew follows Mark, except that the question about fasting is put by the disciples of John the Baptist themselves.

40 · A Sabbath in the Cornfields   Mark 2²³⁻²⁸. Luke 6¹⁻⁵. Matthew 12¹⁻⁸

This was the first of many occasions when Jesus was criticized for his actions on the Sabbath. It has been suggested that he and his disciples were not taking an idle stroll, but were on some missionary journey, and were genuinely hungry. The rubbing together of ears of corn in order to remove the husks was considered by Pharisees to be threshing, and therefore work.

In reply to their criticism Jesus recalled the incident in Scripture when King David had set aside the Law when the needs of his men were more important (I Samuel 21¹⁻⁶). The shewbread, or Bread of the Presence, was specially prepared in twelve loaves and set out in the Holy Shrine. The name of the priest in the David story was Ahimelech, not Abiathar.

In saying that the Sabbath was made for man, Jesus summed up a long history. The origin of the Sabbath seems to have been the need at regular intervals for a day of rest from work, for man, his servants and his animals. Early Sabbath rules were meant to safeguard this need, especially for servants.

Later the Sabbath acquired religious associations with moon-worship in Babylon, where it marked the moon's phases. For Jews, it was associated with God's deliverance of their ancestors from Egypt where they had been slaves. Finally their story of creation gave added religious meaning to the Sabbath for Jews, for God was said to have rested from his work on the Sabbath.

Various explanations are given by scholars in regard to v. 28. (1) Jesus was using the title Son of man to mean himself as Messiah. (2) Jesus was using the term to mean that 'man' was Lord of the Sabbath. (3) v. 28 is some Christian teacher's comment on the story. Since Matthew and Luke omit the statement about man and the Sabbath, explanation 2 is unlikely. Whatever the origins of the Sabbath, it was God's own command that Jews should keep it. Jesus would not be likely to say that 'man' could set aside the command of God. On the other hand, he himself as Son of man might do so.

LUKE. Luke follows Mark, except that he omits *The sabbath was made for man* (as does Matthew). Luke's account favours explanation 1 above.

MATTHEW. Matthew follows Mark, except that he omits *The sabbath was made for man* (as does Luke), and includes a further example of when it is permissible to set aside Sabbath rules (vv. 5 and 6). The requirements of Temple worship were regarded as more important than Sabbath laws, and so priests were exempt from them when carrying out their duties. From this Jesus argued that he, being greater than either David or the Temple, was also exempt.

41 · The Man with the Withered Hand Mark 3¹⁻⁶. Luke 6⁶⁻¹¹. Matthew 12⁹⁻¹⁴

This incident was a further step in the Sabbath controversy. Rabbis allowed medical attention to be given on the Sabbath, if life was in danger. Jesus argued that it was lawful to do good at any time.

Normally Pharisees had nothing to do with Herodians. Now the Pharisees seek their co-operation as representing the civil authorities.

LUKE. Luke follows Mark, but omits the detail that Jesus was angry. Perhaps Luke thought that this was not quite in keeping with Jesus' character, and overlooked that it was righteous anger on behalf of someone else.

MATTHEW. In Matthew, the Pharisees put the question, *Is it lawful to heal on the sabbath day?* and Jesus argues from the Sabbath concession made by some rabbis in respect of an animal in danger. The Herodians are not mentioned, only that the Pharisees *took counsel.*

D

42 · Jesus and Publicity

Mark 3⁷⁻¹². Luke 6¹⁷⁻¹⁹.
Matthew 12¹⁵⁻²¹

The Pharisees had tried to enlist the help of the Herodians, the civil
authorities, in their campaign against Jesus. Consequently he kept out of
their way as much as possible. The sea in v. 7 is the Sea of Galilee. Mark
mentions once again how the unclean spirits recognized the true
identity of Jesus.

LUKE. Luke's somewhat shorter version is used to set the scene for the
Sermon on the Plain.

MATTHEW. Matthew inserts into his narrative the first of the Servant
Songs (Isaiah 42¹⁻⁴). The first verse of the song contains the words spoken
by God at the baptism of Jesus. The point of the quotation here is that,
since official Israel (i.e. Scribes, Pharisees, Herodians) was rejecting the
Messiah and God's revelation, then the mission of God's servant would
be to the Gentiles.

43 · The Appointment of the Twelve

Mark 3¹³⁻¹⁹. Luke 6¹²⁻¹⁶.
Matthew 10²⁻⁴

All the followers of Jesus were disciples (from the Latin *discipulus*, a
scholar or one who learns), but from their number Jesus chose twelve to
be with him constantly, and to receive specialized instruction. The
Twelve are known as apostles (from the Greek *apostello*, I send).

The number was twelve to correspond to the twelve tribes of Israel.
The twelve apostles were to be the beginning of the new Israel, the
Christian Church.

Thaddaeus becomes Judas (Jude) in Luke and Lebbaeus in Matthew.

Principles and Duties

44 · The Sermon on the Mount   Matthew 5, 6, 7. Luke 6$^{20-49}$

Matthew and Luke both got the main subject matter for the sermon from the common source document Q, but, since only some of the sermon in Matthew is to be found in Luke, it is impossible to check how much of the whole, notably the illustrations from Jewish Law, come from document Q or Matthew's own source M.

Both writers place the sermon after the selection by Jesus of the twelve special disciples, but, whereas Matthew collects most of the teaching together according to its subject matter, as though Jesus gave the teaching all on one occasion, Luke keeps some of the teaching for other suitable places in his narrative. Thus Matthew 6$^{5-15}$ comes in Luke 11$^{1-4}$ after Jesus at prayer; Matthew 6$^{25-33}$ comes in Luke 12$^{22-31}$ after the parable of The Rich Fool; Matthew 7$^{7-11}$ comes in Luke 11$^{9-13}$ after the parable of The Friend at Midnight. In doing this Luke more likely has Jesus' teaching in its original settings.

Since Matthew's sermon is compact, the notes following will deal with its contents first, and then with Luke's corresponding verses.

45 · The Scene of the Sermon   Matthew 4$^{23-25}$, 5$^{1-2}$. Luke 6$^{16-19}$

Both Gospels indicate in the verses that precede the sermon that a large company of people followed Jesus, many seeking healing, many to hear him *preaching the gospel of the kingdom.*

The Jewish Law had been given by God to his people through Moses on Mount Sinai. The sermon contains the principles of Christian conduct, and so Matthew presents Jesus as a lawgiver greater than Moses, giving the Christian Law also upon a mountain. As Matthew was writing for Jewish Christians this parallel would be significant.

In Luke the scene of the sermon is merely incidental. Jesus had chosen the Twelve from among his many disciples gathered on a mountain, after which *he came down with them, and stood on a level place.* For this reason Luke's account of the sermon is often referred to as the Sermon on the Plain.

46 · The Beatitudes Matthew 5^{3-12}. Luke 6^{20-26}

In their original Aramaic the Beatitudes are a set of two-lined verses. Even in English they retain something of their rhythm. There are eight Beatitudes in Matthew and four in Luke, the number there being made up by four 'Woes'. The reason for this difference is not known. The word Beatitude comes from a Latin word for happiness.

Each Beatitude begins with the word 'blessed', and describes people who are truly fortunate, not in the way in which worldly people assess good fortune, but as it is regarded by the religiously minded. Taken together the virtues commended in the Beatitudes constitute a unified Christian character. The promises or compensations attached to the Beatitudes differ more in words than in substance. The general meaning is that people who develop these virtues are rewarded with great spiritual blessings.

In Matthew the Beatitudes are addressed to Christians in general, but in Luke apparently to the poor, hungry, oppressed and outcast, actually listening to Jesus at the time. Luke refers the more often to the kingdom of God; Matthew, because of Jewish reverence for the name or title of God, writes rather of the kingdom of heaven.

(1) Matthew 5^3, Luke 6^{20-24}.

By *the poor in spirit* we understand those who are conscious of their lack of spiritual qualities, in contrast with those who imagine that they possess ample spiritual resources of their own. The poor in spirit are the willing and eager recipients of God's grace. Luke applies the Beatitude specifically to those poor financially, and correspondingly adds a 'Woe' against the rich.

(2) Matthew 5^4, Luke $6^{21, 25}$.

Primarily *they that mourn* are people who, like Jesus, grieve for the sins and sorrows of the world, often with their sympathy focused upon individuals. Two examples of such mourning are to be found in the Gospels. Luke 19^{41-44} tells how Jesus wept over Jerusalem, because he foresaw its destruction. John 11^{35} tells how Jesus joined in the grief of Martha and Mary when their brother Lazarus was dead.

But included in such 'mourning' is disquiet about one's own sins, and a desire for amendment. And Luke extends such personal sorrow to cover loss and bereavement.

(3) Matthew 5[5].

This Beatitude is taken from Psalm 37[11]. *The meek* are the unassuming, the unpretentious, the non-arrogant. They are not weak, for, to control a natural tendency towards assertiveness, requires much strength of character; nor are the meek necessarily submissive, for on occasion they have to act vigorously against what is wrong. Thus Jesus himself was meek. When turned away by the Samaritan villagers he checked his own annoyance and that of his disciples (Luke 9[51–56]), but when he saw the Temple being misused he protested strongly.

(4) Matthew 5[6], Luke 6[21, 25].

Righteousness is the state or condition of being right, especially morally. To *hunger and thirst* after righteousness is to long for it intensely, both for oneself and for society. The would-be righteous man desires to be in a state of rightness with God and his fellow-men; he desires also to see society at large in a similar state.

So desiring he endeavours to bring about what he desires, concentrating first upon himself, and then extending his efforts widely. Concentration upon himself does not make him selfish, for only by getting himself right first is he likely to get anyone else right. The effectiveness of Jesus as a social reformer sprang directly from the fact that he was the sort of person that he was.

(5) Matthew 5[7].

The merciful are those who are in a position to hurt others, and yet, as much as possible, refrain from doing so. Such hurting may be in word (e.g. when giving an opinion about someone), or in deed (e.g. when requiring payment of a debt). But being merciful is more than abstention: it is active concern for the unfortunate. Thus we speak of 'works of mercy'. The Good Samaritan 'showed mercy' upon the wounded Jew, by trying to reduce the hurt that he had received (Luke 10[37]).

Jesus made it clear that only the merciful may expect to obtain mercy from God. His teaching on the matter is full of illustrations: e.g. Matthew 6[12] (referred to by Shakespeare in the 'Trial Scene' in *The Merchant of Venice*), Matthew 7[1–5], 18[21–35], 25[31–46].

(6) Matthew 5[8].

The more obvious meaning of *pure in heart* is purity of mind and body, but the word *pure* is often used, as in metallurgy, to mean unalloyed.

Thus the *pure in heart* are those without mixed loyalties or motives, those whose dominating purpose it is to serve God. Such people, so single-minded and *pure in heart*, will attain to their desire, and see God in his holiness.

(7) Matthew 5⁹.

Peace is a word frequently used in the New Testament, and it meant for the first Christians far more than an absence of strife. The Christian idea of peace was expressed in the words of Jesus, *Peace I leave with you; my peace I give unto you; not as the world giveth* . . . (John 14²⁷). Such peace is a calm tranquillity undisturbed by misplaced anxiety. St. Paul lists this kind of peace as one of the fruits of the Holy Spirit (Galatians 5²²).

Those having this inner peace live in harmony with God, with themselves, and with all creation. But they are more than 'peace full': they are peace-makers; they radiate peace to others; they actively seek to bring peace on earth, so that others may live in similar harmony. At the same time the peace-makers avoid being provocative and causing dissension. In this respect they may be thought of as peace-keepers.

God himself is the God of Peace (Philippians 4⁷, ⁹). Peace-makers therefore possess one of the attributes of God, and because they do so may to that extent regard themselves as *sons of God*.

(8) Matthew 5¹⁰.

Jesus warned his followers that they would be persecuted (Mark 13⁹⁻¹³). By the time that Matthew was writing, persecution had become a real experience. Well might he write, *they that have been persecuted*.

(8a) Matthew 5¹¹, Luke 6²².

This Beatitude is a continuation of the previous one, the governing words being *for my sake*. The blessing is for those who would suffer in the cause of righteousness not merely as brave or unfortunate individuals, but because of their personal loyalty to Jesus. Luke makes particular reference to those who had been excommunicated from the synagogues.

(8b) Matthew 5¹², Luke 6²³, ²⁶.

This Beatitude is the climax of the two previous. Persecution was a cause for rejoicing. God's prophets in times past had so suffered. A persecuted Christian was therefore in good company.

47 · The Salt and the Light   Mark 4²¹⁻²³, 9⁵⁰. Luke 8¹⁶⁻¹⁸,
                                   11³³, 14³⁴⁻³⁵. Matthew 5¹³⁻¹⁶

The symbol of light was one that Jews and Gentiles could both readily understand. The oil lamp used in those days was put upon a tall lampstand, so as to give maximum illumination. No one would put it underneath a bushel, that is, a container for dry measuring. In like manner the light of Christian witness needed to be set high, so as to shine into the darkness of the world round about, and attract people by its brilliance.

It is very likely that the Jews had some proverb about flavourless salt, and that Jesus made use of it when describing the need for people to influence for good their worldly surroundings. If people were not exerting that influence, they were as useless as tasteless salt. Salt is a preservative, antiseptic and a flavouring. For the writers of the Gospels this meant that the Christian influence was to work in the world for the preservation of what was good, and the improvement of what was bad.

LUKE. Luke 8¹⁶ says for Gentile readers *that they which enter in may see the light*. Luke was thinking of a Greek or Roman house with a lamp burning in the entrance porch.

MATTHEW. Matthew 5¹⁵ describes how the lamp on its stand *shineth unto all that are in the house* because Matthew was thinking of a Jewish one-roomed house.

The symbol of light had a special significance for Jews. In Jewish literature the expression *light of the world* or *lamp of the world* is fairly common. The Jews had been called by God to be his lamp; he would light it with his glory, for he himself was the light of Israel (Psalm 18²⁸, 27¹, 36⁹). Jerusalem was to be the lampstand of the Divine Light, for the city was the centre of the Jewish religion.

Jerusalem was *a city set on a hill*, and Jesus was probably thinking about it, and the words of Isaiah 2²⁻³ as he pictured the people of all nations flocking to *the mountain of the Lord's house* (the Temple) to learn about God, and going out from Jerusalem to carry forth his Law. Jesus may also have had in mind Isaiah 60¹⁻³.

For Matthew's Jewish Christian readers the symbol of salt also would have particular association. They knew the saying, *The Torah is like salt.* So the words of Jesus would be a reminder to them that the Christian Law must be like salt to them in the same way as the Jewish Law was salt for the Jews, that is, something essential to life (Ecclesiasticus 39²⁶).

It is possible that when these words were spoken by Jesus he was thinking of how the Jews had failed to be salt to the earth. Since the Jews had failed to be salt, just as they had hidden away their light, and the Christian Church had come to regard itself as the New Israel, the Jewish

Christian community for whom Matthew was writing, would find in Jesus' words a double meaning.

48 · The Jewish Law

The term *The Law* was comprehensive.

(1) First it covered the Torah. The core of the Torah was the Ten Commandments given to Moses on Mount Sinai, and the Book of the Covenant, an expansion of those commandments (Exodus 20^{22}-23^{33}). The purpose of the Torah was twofold: *(a)* Religious: to set forth Israel's obligations to God, who had chosen them to be his people, and had entered into solemn covenant with them; *(b)* Social: to set forth the obligations of the people one to another as members of a community, in order to safeguard the needs and rights of individuals.

This recognition of a double duty towards God and man was a unique feature of the Jewish Law. Both its religious and its social obligations were sacred.

(2) The term included also the Mishna, or Oral Law. This was built up from the traditions of the scribes, the lawyers who studied the Torah, and sought to apply it to everyday life. For example, the Law would not allow work on the Sabbath (Exodus 20^{9-11}). But what was work? This the scribes defined.

(3) The term included the Talmud, which consisted of written laws based on the oral tradition, which eventually came to be written down.

49 · Jesus' Attitude Towards the Jewish Law   Matthew 5^{17-20}
(cf. Luke 16^{17})

The Law of Moses was the most sacred part of the Jewish Scriptures, and next in esteem were the writings of the prophets. The attitude of Jesus towards the Law was an important matter for Jewish Christians. Matthew, therefore, was anxious to show how loyal Jesus was towards it. As the subject did not worry Gentile Christians, there is less stress upon it in Mark and Luke.

Jesus' attitude is summed up in Matthew 5^{17}, *Think not that I came to destroy the law or the prophets: I came not to destroy, but to fulfil.* The word *fulfil* seems here to be used in two ways:

(1) Jesus brought out the deeper teaching of the Law and the prophets. Hitherto only the surface meanings had been heeded. The Sermon on the Mount gives specific examples of how Jesus fulfilled the Law in this way.

(2) Jesus adequately satisfied the Jewish Messianic hope. So in this

sense also he could claim to fulfil all that the Law and the prophets had to say about the coming Messiah. Luke records that after his resurrection Jesus explained to the Twelve *how that all things must needs be fulfilled, which are written in the law of Moses, and the prophets, and the psalms, concerning me* (Luke 24²⁷, ⁴⁴). This had been the significance of the appearance of Moses and Elijah at the transfiguration. It is in this connection that Matthew uses the word *fulfil* when he writes about prophetic utterances as actually coming true.

V. 18 can be interpreted in either of two ways:

(1) To mean that not even the smallest obligation of the Law could be ignored *till all things be accomplished,* i.e. till the kingdom of God had come.

(2) To mean that all that was expected in the Law and the prophets concerning the Messiah must be accomplished before they could pass away. Jewish Christians, like St. Paul, came to regard the Law as having passed away with the coming of Jesus, its purpose having been served.

Till heaven and eath pass away recalls the belief of Jewish rabbis that, though everything has an end, including heaven and earth, the one thing that has no end is the divine Law (cf. Luke 16¹⁷, where these words refer to the Law and not to prophecy; and Mark 13³¹, where it is the words of Jesus that remain when all else has come to an end).

Jot and *tittle* translate the Greek words *iota* and *keraia*. *Iota* is the name of the smallest letter in the Greek alphabet; *keraia* means a horn. (Jot is derived from *iota*. The derivation of tittle is uncertain.) The Jewish Law was, of course, written in Hebrew. So the words of Jesus referred in some way to the Law as it was written down. Probably therefore *iota*, the smallest Greek letter, represents *yodh*, the smallest Hebrew letter, and *keraia*, meaning horn, represents small hooks or strokes used in Hebrew writing.

Had Jesus been speaking English, and referring to the English written law, he might well have said that neither the dot on the letter i nor the cross on the letter t was to be omitted from it. In this stress on the importance of detail in the Jewish Law Jesus was thinking narrowly of the Torah.

The *righteousness of the scribes and Pharisees* mentioned ironically in v. 20 was a self-satisfaction that resulted from the keeping of the Oral Law as well.

Jesus never questioned the divine authority of the Torah. He was loyal to it, and, as Matthew shows in the Sermon on the Mount, he wished people to remember the original purpose of it, which was to serve and not enslave.

The clashes that Jesus had with the scribes and Pharisees concerned the Oral Law (Mark 3¹⁻⁶, Luke 13¹¹⁻¹⁷). They criticized Jesus for ignoring it, and he criticized them (*a*) for getting so lost in legal details that they forgot the essential spirit of the Law, (*b*) for maintaining ceremonial customs while disregarding their meaning (Mark 7$^{1-7}$), (*c*) for permitting the Oral Law in some cases to make mockery of the Torah (Mark 7$^{8-13}$).

Thus Jesus' attitude towards the whole Law was governed by its original twofold purpose. If the work of God or human need was likely to suffer restriction because of some part of the Law, then the work of God or human need was the more urgent. Jesus' acts of healing on the Sabbath were both the work of God and a satisfaction of human need. Jews believed that sickness originated with the devil; so, for the Jews, every act of healing by Jesus was intended to demonstrate a weakening of the grip of evil on the world, and an extension of God's kingdom.

50 · Five Examples from the Law of Moses   Matthew 5$^{21-48}$

Matthew, writing for Jewish Christians, includes in his 'sermon' five examples of how the teaching of Jesus fulfilled the Law of Moses by revealing its deeper meanings. Each example begins with the words *Ye have heard that it was said*. Then the Law is quoted, and Jesus continues, *but I say unto you*, so revealing the fuller implication.

For Jewish Christians in particular these words of Jesus were significant. He was himself claiming the right to revise the sacred Law, the God-given Law! No ordinary Jew would dare to do that.

Example 1. Murder (Matthew 5$^{21-26}$, Luke 12$^{58-59}$)

The reference is to Exodus 20^{13}. The judgement was that of the Supreme Jewish Council, the Sanhedrin, or the Local Council of thirteen members. While the Jewish Law condemned the act of murder, Jesus condemned also the angry thought and word which, if allowed to go unchecked, might lead to murder. The angry person, he implied, was also liable to a judgement, not that of a legal court, but of God.

Some abusive language, such as the use of the term *Raca*, meaning 'empty-head', was an offence that could also be dealt with either by the Local or the Supreme Council. Scholars are uncertain as to whether *Thou fool* is an expression of lesser, equal, or greater contempt than *Raca*. However, Jesus seems to be teaching that, as all anger is sinful, so all terms of abuse or contempt, whether lesser or greater, are sinful.

The *hell of fire* or the *Gehenna of fire* was a term for eternal punishment, and was drived from the continually smouldering rubbish dump in the Valley of Hinnom, to the south of Jerusalem. Once it had been a place where human beings were burned as sacrifices to the god Moloch, but, when this was prohibited by King Josiah, the shrine was defiled and the rubbish dump took its place.

Vv. 23–26 contain two examples of the harm that anger can cause. First, anger is an obstacle to the sincere worship of God. People (*brother* is used in the widest sense) who have quarrelled need to be reconciled with one another before approaching God in worship. Second, anger, if permitted to go unrestrained, may lead a person into situations from which there is no escape (cf. Luke 12$^{58-59}$).

Example 2. Adultery (Matthew 5$^{27-32}$)

The reference is to Exodus 20^{14}. The punishment for adultery was death by stoning (Deuteronomy 22$^{22-24}$). The Law thus condemned the act of adultery, but Jesus condemned also the lustful thought, which, if permitted to go unchecked, might lead to adultery.

Vv. 29 and 30 are a dramatic way of emphasizing the need for stern self-discipline.

Jewish Law allowed divorce (Deuteronomy, 24$^{1-4}$), but Jesus pointed out that this Law caused the breaking of another, because it forced a woman to commit adultery if she married again, and her new husband also to become guilty (see Section 105).

Example 3. Oaths (Matthew 5$^{33-37}$)

The Jewish Law said, *Thou shalt not take the name of the Lord thy God in vain*, that is, to no purpose (Exodus 20^7). The punishment [for irreverence towards God (i.e. blasphemy) was death by stoning. Jews, however, in their frequent use of oaths in everyday speech, habitually took God's name *in vain*, for their oaths often involved his name (cf. Leviticus 19^{12}, Numbers 30^2, Deuteronomy 23^{21}), or something associated with him, e.g. heaven or Jerusalem. The rabbis even distinguished between oaths that had to be kept, and oaths that could be broken (see Matthew 23$^{16-22}$).

So Jesus condemned the spirit of untruthfulness that made oaths necessary. In such cases, oaths sworn by God were irreverent, and oaths sworn by anything else (e.g. the head) were useless. People known always to speak the truth could always be believed.

Example 4. Revenge (Matthew 5$^{38-42}$, Luke 6$^{29-30}$)

The reference is to Exodus 21^{24}, Leviticus 24^{20}, Deuteronomy 19^{21}. The purpose of the Law was to limit revenge to the extent of an offence. By the time of Jesus money payments were exacted by way of compensation. But while the Law thus limited revenge, Jesus forbade it altogether.

The illustrations of this teaching that follow in vv. 39–42 show that

Jesus saw nothing weak in the acceptance of injuries. To restrain oneself from retaliation is evidence of strength. As soon as a person who has been wronged retaliates, he sinks to the level of the aggressor. Sometimes an offender's only motive for inflicting harm upon a person is the desire to provoke him to retaliate, so that the offender may have the satisfaction of seeing his victim fall.

Restraint also can have very positive results. Jesus put his own teaching into practice during his trials, and won the respect of Pilate. Early Christian martyrs followed their master's example, and sometimes so far aroused the sympathy and admiration of judges and spectators as to result in their conversion.

In Palestine a man's coat was his main garment, and his cloak the outer garment worn over it as a protection against the weather. For a peasant it was also his covering at night. This example of the spirit of non-resistance comes from legal proceedings, and indicates a willingness to let an enemy have all that he asks for in court, and more if necessary. It is very likely that this sort of situation was not infrequent among the early Christians. There were plenty of hostile heathens ready to make trouble for them in a court of law.

Unfortunately some Christians also were prepared to sue other Christians in heathen courts. In such cases the less trouble made by the one being sued the better for the good name of the Christian community. St. Paul had to write to Christians at Corinth about this sort of thing. His advice was *Why not rather take wrong? why not rather be defrauded?* (I Corinthians 6¹⁻⁹).

In Roman-occupied Palestine, a Roman soldier could compel or impress any Jew to carry his pack for a mile, or demand the use of his ass for a purpose similar. In this way Simon of Cyrene was compelled to help the Romans by carrying the cross for Jesus. Here the teaching of Jesus suggests that a readiness to do more than the minimum required is a desirable attitude on the part of those who wish to belong to the kingdom.

Luke, in 6²⁹, is very similar to Matthew, except that he omits the quotation from the Jewish Law, since this would not be helpful to his Gentile readers, and changes the taking of coat and cloak from a lawsuit, where they are surrendered, to an act of robbery in which they are stolen.

Example 5. Love (Matthew 5⁴³⁻⁴⁸, Luke 6²⁷⁻²⁸, ³²⁻³⁶)

The reference is to Leviticus 19¹⁸, ³⁴. The Law contained no direct command to *hate thine enemy*, but, since the Jews regarded themselves as God's chosen people, their enemies were regarded as God's enemies, and it was quite permissible to hate them. The Jewish Law thus limited the obligation to love to fellow-Jews, and to those Gentiles who were converts to the Jewish religion.

The command *Love your enemies* often arouses misunderstanding, owing to the fact that the word 'love' in English can have a variety of meanings. Greek-speaking Jews and Christians tried to distinguish between different types of love. Emotional love they referred to as *eros*, from the name of Eros the god of love, and the brotherly love of a person for his friends and fellow-men they called *agape*. It is the Greek *agape* that is translated as 'love' in this passage.

The first Christians made much use of this term. It signified the love of God for them, their love for one another, and their attitude towards the rest of the world.

The basic definition of any sort of love might well be 'the desiring of what is best for someone else'. This kind of love can be given to all, whether they be friend or enemy, and whether one likes or dislikes them. Jesus' own example is the best illustration of this. When he prayed for those who crucified him, he was loving them, not with any warm emotional love, but with a love that wished them no harm, and desired that they might be forgiven.

This, says Jesus, is the way to love as God loves, for his goodness does not discriminate between those who are good and those who are evil. Consequently he enjoins, *Ye therefore shall be perfect, as your heavenly Father is perfect.*

Luke includes more examples than does Matthew of people who restrict their love to those who can return it. To Matthew's *pray for them that persecute you* Luke adds, *do good to them that hate you*, thus emphasizing the need not merely to endure injury but actively to return good for evil. The Jews themselves had a proverb, largely overlooked by them, but quoted by St. Paul in Romans 12[20], in connection with the heaping of coals on an enemy's head.

51 · Religious Duties

Matthew 6[1-18]

Matthew 5 is concerned mainly with the social obligations of the Law. The Law, however, emphasized a double obligation, religious as well as social, and so in Chapter 6 Matthew follows on Jesus' teaching about social obligations with teaching about religious duties. In these also the inner thought was as important as the outward action. V. 1 sums up this teaching. The verses following apply it to three specific religious duties.

(1) The first is almsgiving. This must be done as secretly as possible. Jesus used a well-known proverb for secrecy, *Let not thy left hand know*

what thy right hand doeth. Sounding a trumpet has been from early times, and still is, a metaphor for 'attracting attention'. The word translated 'hypocrite' is itself 'hypocrite' in the Greek Testament. Originally it meant an actor. In the Greek theatre actors portrayed various characters by wearing masks. Consequently the word came to mean someone who gives the impression that he is different from what he really is, and was so used by Jesus.

(2) The second duty is prayer. Here too the right motive must be to give glory to God, not to show off before others. Those who wished to be seen had received their reward in the form of admiration for their apparent sanctity. Jews usually stood when at prayer in the synagogue. Those unable to attend the synagogue at the usual hours of prayer could pray wherever they happened to be.

The *inner chamber* can mean either a private room, thus taking the words literally, or the spiritual withdrawal of the soul in prayer and meditation.

Jesus also warns against the *vain and empty repetitions* used by the heathen Gentiles. The prayers that they used consisted mainly of incantations and meaningless words frequently repeated. No conscious thought was required while the words were being recited.

(At this point Matthew records the Lord's Prayer.)

(3) The third duty is fasting. The bodily discipline of fasting has formed an important part of all great religions. When Jews fasted from food it was customary to put ashes on the head, and to look gloomy and dishevelled for others to see. Jesus taught that special effort should be made to keep fasting secret, otherwise its spiritual blessings would be lost.

It is very likely that, when Jesus was condemning these forms of religious display, he was thinking particularly of the special services that were held during the time of the autumn droughts. These services, which included prayers for rain, were held in the streets. The sounding of ram's horn trumpets, together with public almsgiving and fasting, formed a prominent feature of the services.

Jesus did not condemn any of these religious duties themselves, but only a wrong motive in performing them. almsgiving can, of course, be interpreted widely to include all forms of helping others. For Jews 'almsgiving' and 'righteousness' became almost interchangeable terms.

Jesus said nothing against people meeting together for prayer in a place of worship. He himself always took part in the public worship of the synagogues. A building for 'public' worship is in effect an 'inner chamber' to which people can retire in 'private' or in 'secret' in order to worship God. The principle of secrecy does not exclude the corporate performance of religious obligations by a company of people like-minded, but the motive must still be to give glory to God, and not to show off, even before fellow-members of a congregation.

52 · The Lord's Prayer Matthew 6$^{9-15}$. Luke 11$^{1-4}$

Matthew incorporates the Lord's Prayer in the Sermon on the Mount, but Luke says that Jesus was at prayer when the disciples asked him to teach them to pray. It was not unusual for Jewish rabbis to compose a special pattern prayer for their disciples to use.

The Lord's Prayer can be divided into two parts. The first is a request that God's name may be hallowed (or reverenced), that his kingdom may come, that his will may be done, as in heaven so on earth. The second part contains petitions for daily needs to be supplied, for forgiveness, for mitigation of temptation, and for deliverance from evil. The plural pronouns show that the prayer came to be the prayer of the Christian community rather than of the individual.

The doxology in the Authorized Version of Matthew is absent from the best authorities, and whether it was added to the prayer by Jesus himself or sometime later is uncertain. But such doxologies were not unknown (see I Chronicles 29^{11}), and Jesus could well have used or compiled one.

53 · Contrasts Matthew 6$^{19-34}$. Luke 11$^{34-36}$, 12$^{22-31}$, 12$^{33-34}$, 16^{13}

The remaining part of Matthew 6 contains a series of contrasts between the spiritual and the worldly. Whereas Matthew has grouped all these sayings of Jesus together into one sermon, Luke has made a different use of them.

(1) *Treasure, earthly and heavenly* (Matthew 6$^{19-21}$, Luke 12$^{33-34}$).

Jesus makes two points here. First that earthly treasure is never lasting. Second that a man's main interest dominates his thoughts. In Jewish circles heavenly treasure consisted of good works. The word *rust*, although it is an apt one for deterioration, describes in the Greek 'eating away' not by rust but by such creatures as mice. Jesus was probably thinking of a man who hoarded both fabrics and grain. Moth could prey upon fabrics and 'rust' could prey upon both. Thieves could break through the mud and plaster walls of an Eastern house fairly easily.

(2) *Light and darkness* (Matthew 6$^{22-23}$, Luke 11$^{34-36}$).

The contrast here is between physical and spiritual light and darkness.

49

The eye is the physical source of light for the body. If it fails, physical blindness is the result. *The light that is in thee* is the inner light of spiritual vision. If that light fails, *how great is the darkness*!

An 'evil eye' was a Jewish metaphor for someone who had a grudging heart; a 'good eye' or a 'single eye' meant someone generous-hearted.

(3) *God and mammon* (Matthew 6²⁴, Luke 16¹³).

This is about the impossibility of divided loyalties. *Mammon* was a word meaning any kind of riches.

(4) *Trust and anxiety* (Matthew 6²⁵⁻³⁴, Luke 12²²⁻³²).

It is not sensible foresight that Jesus warns against here, but the anxiety that becomes an obsession. The person who is distracted by worry about what the future may bring is showing a lack of trust in God, who provides for even the least of his creatures. The *lilies of the field* are the anemones that grow wild in Palestine. Dried grass was used as fuel.

In particular these words of Jesus apply to the person who is completely absorbed in material possessions. Jesus points out that such anxiety is useless. *Which of you by being anxious can add one cubit unto his stature?* A cubit varied between 21 and 25 inches.

Matthew 6³³ sums up Jesus' teaching about trust and anxiety. It is all a matter of priorities. The person who puts God first will find that other things fall into place. Matthew 6³⁴ means that there are enough troubles in the present without worrying about those in the future.

54 · Judging Others   Matthew 7¹⁻⁶. Luke 6³⁷⁻⁴² (Mark 4²⁴⁻²⁵)

The teaching here is that only those who are generous in judging or criticizing others, in forgiving others, and in showing mercy, are in the right inward state to receive God's generosity. It is quite possible that, when Matthew wrote these words, he had particularly in mind the unseemly practice of some Christians to sue one another, or their enemies, in the heathen courts of law (see Section 50 at p. 46).

Luke's picture of generosity is a measure of corn full to overflowing. The folds of a man's garment, if it was tied at the waist, could be used as a large bag.

The picture of a mote (some tiny particle) and a beam was a familiar one among Jews to describe a readiness to judge others.

55 · Pearls before Swine   Matthew 7⁶

Dogs were generally despised; for the most part they ran wild and

served as scavengers along the streets. According to the Law swine were
'unclean'. So *dogs* and *swine* were terms of contempt and abuse (cf.
II Peter 2²²). *That which is holy* would refer to the foods reserved for
consumption by priests. Pearls would be useless as food for pigs, so the
hungry animals would turn upon their keepers.

It is possible that Matthew records this cautionary saying here in
order to balance what might be called the indiscriminate trustfulness
enjoined in the preceding verses. By his time the Christian Church
suffered both hostility from Jews and misunderstanding from Gentiles,
all of whom were ready to distort and misrepresent Christian teaching.

Mark (in 6⁷⁻¹³) records similar advice from Jesus about the use of
discretion in presenting his message.

56 · Persistence in Prayer   Matthew 7⁷⁻¹¹. Luke 11⁵⁻¹³

MATTHEW. Matthew 7⁷⁻⁸ contains another example of how Jesus, in
common with Jewish rabbis, taught his disciples in verse form. Jesus
argues that, if a human father, prone to evil, can give good gifts to his
children, God is unlikely to give anything less than the best to his
children.

LUKE. Luke, who puts *Holy Spirit* in place of *good things*, introduces
this teaching about persistence in prayer with the parable of The Friend
at Midnight. The picture is of a man and his family lying on their bed-
mats on the floor of their one-roomed house. A friend comes to borrow
some bread. Jewish hospitality was such that a traveller could call at a
house at any hour of day or night and ask for food and lodging. The
friend in the parable had been so called upon, but, not having in store
sufficient bread with which to feed his visitor, appeals to his neighbour.

His neighbour, the head of the family gone to bed, is not pleased at
being so called upon. If he answers the door, he will disturb his family;
if he does not, the knocking will waken them anyway. So, says Jesus,
*Though he will not rise and give him because he is his friend, yet because of
his importunity he will.* (Luke 18¹⁻⁸ illustrates the same point.)

57 · The Golden Rule   Matthew 7¹². Luke 6³¹

Jesus sums up all the teaching in the Law and the prophets in a positive
command, to do actual good, not merely to refrain from evil.

The negative principle of refraining from doing evil to others was well
known in the time of Jesus. The great Chinese philosopher Confucius,

E   *51*

living 500 years before Christ, taught it, and many later philosophers echoed his words. The renowed Jewish rabbi Hillel recalled them, saying, 'That which thou hatest do not to thy fellow; this is the whole law.'

The 'do as you would be done by' teaching of Jesus expressed a nobler, because more positive, principle.

58 · The Two Ways   Matthew 7[13-14]. Luke 13[22-30]

MATTHEW. The idea that man is faced with a choice between the two ways of life and death is frequent in Jewish literature (Deuteronomy 30[19], Jeremiah 21[8], Ecclesiasticus 2[12], 15[17]).

In Matthew's account of Jesus' words, the picture is of a gate leading to a path, or way, of life. The teaching is not that God intends only a few people to find salvation, but that only a few people, by comparison, are prepared to make the effort necessary to find the path, and, having found it, to keep to it. The way to destruction demands no effort, is much more attractive, and therefore very much more popular.

The two ways, based on these words of Jesus, are a frequent theme in later Christian writings.

LUKE. Instead of a gate leading to a path, Luke describes a door leading to a banqueting room. The allusion comes in answer to the question, *Lord, are there few that be saved?* Jesus and the Twelve were on the last journey to Jerusalem, and there is great urgency in the words of Jesus as Luke reports them. A banquet was a familiar symbolic picture of the Messianic kingdom.

59 · False Teachers   Matthew 7[15-20]. Luke 6[43-45]

With the continued spread of Christianity, the number of missionary teachers was ever increasing. These teachers, like the great St. Paul, were continually travelling from place to place. This gave opportunity for vagabonds, posing as Christian teachers or prophets, to impose upon unsuspecting Christians, who gave them hospitality.

Some Christian writings warned against such people. Here was given a clue to their genuineness. If a stranger, claiming to be a Christian prophet, asked for elaborate hospitality and money, and attempted to stay for more than two days, then the 'prophet' was probably a fraud.

60 · The Parable of the Two Foundations   Matthew 7²¹⁻²⁹. Luke 6⁴⁶⁻⁴⁹

The Sermon on the Mount ends with Jesus stressing the truth that the wise man is he who acts upon this teaching. His faith will endure like a house built on a rock. It is not sufficient merely to profess belief in Jesus. Faith, unsupported by right conduct, is like a house built on sand.

The parable here is a further example of the use of verse form. Vv. 25 and 27 carry the refrain. V. 27 has a dramatic change in the last line. (The poetry is not so obvious in Luke.)

A saying of Jewish rabbis is probably the basis of the parable. They compared a man who had learned much Torah, and who did many good works, with a man who, though he had learned much Torah, did no good works. This sort of teaching goes back to the great prophets whose constant theme was that acts of worship without righteousness of life were unacceptable to God (cf. the parable of The Sheep and the Goats, Matthew 25³¹⁻⁴⁶).

With v. 28 Matthew concludes |his first book of teaching. His other four books are concluded in a similar way (11¹, 13⁵³, 19¹, 26¹).

61 · The Conclusion of the Sermon

Matthew in the 'sermon' has made an anthology of Jesus' teaching. He mentions *the multitude* at the beginning and end of his First Book of Teaching (see section 12), in order to give the sermon a typical Palestinian setting, but Matthew is really re-directing the teaching of Jesus towards the early Christian community.

The teaching contained in the sermon deals with the principles of conduct. It does not aim at prescribing the right course of conduct in particular situations. Had this been so, it would soon have been out of date. The principles of conduct contained in the sermon are timeless: humility, mercy (which forgives others, and abstains from criticizing), singleness of purpose, a longing for goodness (which is more than a legal observance), a striving for peace, a willingness to suffer for what is right without desire for revenge, control of temper, moral purity, truth in speech, sincerity in religious duties, and finally trust in God's care.

Healing and Teaching

62 · The Centurion's Servant
Luke 7$^{1-10}$. Matthew 8$^{5-13}$

LUKE. The healing of the centurion's servant is notable for three reasons: Jesus healed a Gentile; he healed without meeting the sick servant; he made special comment upon the centurion's great faith.

The centurion was so named because he commanded a hundred men. In sending the elders he may have thought that Jesus, like any other strict Jew, would be unwilling to meet a Gentile. He certainly had no wish, and saw no need, for Jesus to be embarrassed in his house. He recognized Jesus as a person who, like himself, had but to command to be obeyed.

MATTHEW. Matthew's story is shorter. He leaves out the commendation of the centurion by the Jewish elders. The centurion comes himself to make his request. Matthew adds vv. 11 and 12. The Messianic kingdom is described in the familiar Jewish fashion as a banquet.

63 · The Widow's Son
Luke 7$^{11-17}$

The city of Nain, now a little village, is situated in Galilee about twenty-five miles south-west of Capernaum. Its name means 'fair', and it is reached by a rocky pathway leading up the hillside.

The widow's situation was doubly sad: she would have no one to support her, and she would now be regarded as a childless widow who had lost God's favour. By touching the bier Jesus ignored the ceremonial law which said that by touching the dead, or any thing in contact with the dead, a person became conventionally unclean.

The people who felt that a great prophet had arisen among them could scarcely help remembering how two great prophets were said to have raised the dead: Elijah (I Kings 17) and Elisha (II Kings 4). Shunem was only two miles away from Nain.

54

In the Synoptic Gospels this is the only recorded miracle of raising the dead other than that of Jairus's daughter.

64 · John the Baptist's Question

Luke 7^{18-35}, 16^{16}.
Matthew 11^{1-19}

According to the Jewish historian Josephus, John was imprisoned in the fortress of Machaerus on the shores of the Dead Sea.

John's messengers reached Jesus as he was engaged in works of healing. He did not send back a direct answer but spoke of what he was doing in words that would remind John of Isaiah 35^{5-6} and 61^1. Thus he pointed out to John that his work was indeed that expected of the Messiah.

V. 27 refers to Malachi 3^1, containing the words with which Mark introduced John the Baptist at the beginning of his Gospel. Possibly they were one of the numerous proof-texts from Jewish Scriptures used by Christian teachers to show that John was the Messianic herald.

John was the last of the long line of prophets, and, although his story comes in the New Testament, his outlook and his knowledge of God really belong to the Old Testament. He died when Jesus' work had only recently begun. Therefore the humblest Christian, with all the advantages of Jesus' revelation of God, was greater, or rather more privileged, than John the Baptist.

Vv. 29 and 30 tell how many listening to Jesus had been baptized by John, and how many others had rejected his message. To illustrate the attitude of some Jews to John and to himself, Jesus spoke of children playing in the market-place. Whether their game was 'weddings' or 'funerals' there were often some who did not wish to play. Similarly neither John's life of self-denial, nor Jesus' ordinary eating and drinking, was approved of.

In v. 35 Wisdom is personified, and her true children are those who act wisely, particularly in their attitude towards John and Jesus.

MATTHEW. Matthew's account comes from the same source as Luke's. V. 12 is difficult. The kingdom of heaven could be thought of as subjected to violence in two ways: by people eager to belong to it; or by people hostile to it, and attacking it. In support of the first there is Luke 16^{16}, where *every man* is an obvious exaggeration. In support of the second there is the fact that since John's execution there had come Jesus' crucifixion, followed by the persecution of his followers.

Vv. 13–14 recognize John as fulfilling the prophecy in Malachi 4^5: he was the Elijah who was to return to herald the coming of the Messiah.

55

65 · The Sinful Woman
Luke 7³⁶–8³

In inviting Jesus to dine with him, Simon possibly thought that the presence of a prophet would provide a certain amount of interest for his other guests. Those of his own social standing he welcomed in the customary way. As each guest entered the sandals were removed, and dusty feet were washed. The host then greeted his guests with a kiss, and the salutation, 'Peace be with you'. As a mark of special honour, perfumed oil was applied to the hair. Jesus received no such courtesies.

Richer Jews, especially in the towns, had adopted the Roman practice of reclining for meals on wide divans set around a table. Feasts held by rich people were never very private affairs: any who wished to do so might stand and watch. The woman was more than a *sinner* in the technical sense of the word, meaning someone who made no attempt to keep the Law of Moses. It is very likely that she was a prostitute, who, having heard Jesus' teaching, felt remorse for her past life. Doubtless Simon thought that Jesus was not much of a prophet, if he did not realize what sort of woman this was.

The parable of The Two Debtors is one of gratitude for forgiveness, and receives practical application in vv. 44–50. The woman had repented, and had been forgiven. Notice *are forgiven* in v. 47. In v. 48 Jesus reassured her of this. *She loved much* in v. 47 referred apparently to the quality of her penitence. 8¹⁻³ mentions some women who ministered to Jesus and his disciples. (It was not unusual for wealthy women to provide financial support for rabbis.) Some gave their help in gratitude for having been healed by Jesus. In particular there was Mary of Magdala, or *Mary that was called Magdalene*. Her affliction had probably been some mental illness.

Christian tradition has identified Mary Magdalene with the sinful woman in Simon's house (it being assumed that the demons that possessed her showed themselves in an evil way of life, instead of in the more usual madness). But also she has been identified with the unknown woman in Mark 14³, and with Mary of Bethany in John 12³. In view of the similarities, some scholars think that Luke's story is but his version of the Bethany anointing. (See Section 125.)

All that is known for certain about Mary Magdalene is that she was healed by Jesus, and supported his work financially, that she stood by the cross (John 19²⁵), that she was one of the women who visited the tomb (Mark 16¹), and that she was the first person to see the risen Jesus (Mark 16⁹⁻¹⁰, John 20¹¹⁻¹⁸).

66 · The Sin Against the Holy Spirit

Mark 3^{22-30}. Luke 11^{14-32}.
Matthew $12^{22-37, \ 43-45}$
(9^{32-34})

Since there was no denying that Jesus worked miracles, especially those of exorcism (casting out demons) the scribes accused him of being in league with the devil. Two names are given for the chief demon, Satan and Beelzebub. A more accurate transliteration from the Greek is Beezeboul, meaning 'lord of dung' or 'lord of the dwelling' (i.e. the dwelling of the demons). Beelzebub or Baal-zebub was the name of the god of the Philistine city of Ekron.

The point of v. 23 is that Jews believed that sickness was the work of the devil. Would Satan undo his own work? In the parable in v. 27 the strong man is the devil, and the stronger is Jesus. In vv. 28–30 blasphemy against the Holy Spirit seems to consist of speaking of good as evil (as the scribes had been doing). It cannot be forgiven because it is a deliberate reversal of moral standards.

LUKE. Luke introduces his account with an actual exorcism. In v. 19 Jesus points out that some Jews attempted exorcism (Tobit 8^{1-4}, Acts 19^{13}). In v. 20 he claims for his own exorcizing that it was a sign that the kingdom of God was already taking shape. In v. 23 he asserts that in the fight against evil there can be no neutrality.

For vv. 27–28 see Section 68.

MATTHEW. Matthew introduces his account with the healing of a blind and dumb demoniac. The people were so impressed that they wondered whether Jesus was the Messiah, i.e. Son of David. The Pharisees could not allow such ideas to circulate (cf. Matthew 9^{32-34} – possibly a duplicate account).

Vv. 33–37 condemn the Pharisees for pretending a concern for what was right when they did not truly feel any.

MATTHEW (vv. 43–45), LUKE (vv. 24–26). Both Matthew and Luke include a parable of The Unclean Spirits, as a warning of the possibility of moral lapse, especially through self-confidence. Dry, waterless places were thought of as favourite abodes of demons. Jesus may have been commenting upon how the Jews, freed by God from heathen superstition, had put little positive good in its place, or upon how, after their initial response to his preaching, they had degenerated into indifference or opposition.

67 · The Demand for a Sign

Mark 8[11-13]. Luke 11[29-32], 12[54-57]. Matthew 12[38-42], 16[1-4]

This demand was a repetition of the temptation in the wilderness to employ the spectacular. Possibly Jesus' opponents had in mind the story of Elijah's calling down fire from heaven on the worshippers of Baalzebub (II Kings 1).

LUKE. The *sign of Jonah* refers to the mission of the prophet Jonah described in the book of that name in the Old Testament. Jonah was a warning sign to the people of Nineveh. In like manner Jesus was a warning sign to the Jewish nation. The Queen of the South was the Queen of Sheba (the modern Yemen).

Some scholars suggest that the comparison in this account was originally, not between Jonah (or Solomon) and Jesus, but between Jonah and John the Baptist, who even then, as Jonah did, was preaching repentance, and winning Jesus' admiration (Luke 7[28]). The words of Jesus in v. 32 were the more forceful because the commended Ninevites were Gentiles.

MATTHEW. In Luke Jesus refers to the people of his day as an evil generation. Matthew adds the word adulterous, an Old Testament term meaning unfaithful to God.

In v. 40 Matthew is thinking of the three days between Jesus' death and resurrection, during which time he was in the realm of departed spirits, Sheol, thought to be in the heart of the earth.

68 · The Relatives of Jesus

Mark 3[20, 21, 31-35]. Luke 8[19-21], 11[27, 28]. Matthew 12[46-50]

In connection with the Beelzebub controversy Mark mentions the concern of the friends and brethren of Jesus about the state of his mind. Who were these brethren?

They are named in Mark 6[3] as James, Joses, Judas and Simon. Some sisters also are mentioned. During the ministry of Jesus they were opposed to him, but after the resurrection they became disciples (Acts 1[14]). *James, the Lord's brother*, although not an apostle, became leader of the Church in Jerusalem, and presided at the first council there (Acts 15). Perhaps he was chosen because the Twelve, being Jews, were influenced by the fact that the Jewish high priesthood was kept within a family. James was followed by Simon.

These relatives of Jesus may have been:

(1) Children of Mary, born after Jesus, and therefore in that sense

brothers and sisters. Against this is the ancient Christian tradition that Jesus was Mary's only child, and two Bible statements *(a)* that, during the childhood of Jesus, Mary was so free from child-bearing as to be able to make repeated visits to Jerusalem (Luke 2⁴¹), *(b)* that when Jesus was crucified Mary was not committed to the care of any child of her own.

(2) Step-brothers, children of Joseph by a former wife whose death had left him a widower. Tradition makes Joseph much older than Mary, because he seems to have died before Jesus' ministry began. (On the other hand his death could have been due to illness and not to age.)

(3) Cousins, the word brethren being used in a sense wider than is usual with us (Genesis 13⁸, Exodus 2¹¹, I Corinthians 15⁶).

LUKE. Luke 8¹⁹⁻²¹ follows Mark 3³¹⁻³⁵. In Luke 11²⁷, ²⁸ a woman in the crowd said that Mary was blessed in having such a son. 'Blessed is thy mother' was a Jewish greeting. Jesus did not reject the woman's compliment but made it more inclusive. *Yea, rather* might be translated as 'So too'.

MATTHEW. Matthew follows Mark.

69 · Things New and Old   Mark 4³³⁻³⁴. Matthew 13⁵¹⁻⁵²

Mark ends his selection of parables, and distinguishes between Jesus' public teaching and private instruction.

MATTHEW. Matthew ends his collection of parables of the kingdom. No one is quite sure of the meaning of the words. Possibly they mean that every Jewish scribe who became a disciple of Jesus, and therefore is instructed in the mystery of the kingdom of heaven, has double treasure to draw upon: old treasure, in the history of God's revelation to the Jews, and new treasure, in his revelation of himself in Jesus.

70 · The Murdered Galileans   Luke 13¹⁻⁹

Even though the book of Job rejected the idea, it was commonly supposed that calamity was God's punishment for individual sins. Presumably the Galileans were nationalists, and caused a disturbance. The Roman fortress of Antonia, or Tower of Antony, was situated at one corner of the Temple precincts, and at any sign of disturbance the Roman garrison on duty could immediately enter the Temple. The eighteen workmen were engaged in constructing the aqueduct designed by Pilate to bring water to Jerusalem.

Jesus rejected the idea that individual misfortune is always the direct result of individual sin. Nevertheless he added a stern warning that the entire nation was heading for disaster, unless it repented. The warning was further expressed in the parable of The Fruitless Fig Tree. A vineyard was an ancient symbol for the Jewish nation. A fruitless fig tree in a vineyard was doubly out of place. Not only was it unfruitful, but it cumbered the ground (i.e. made it sterile and prevented other things from growing).

Some scholars believe this parable to be the basis of the story of the cursing of the fig tree that appears in Mark 11$^{12-14}$ and Matthew 21$^{18-21}$ (see Section 115).

71 · The Crippled Woman   Luke 13$^{10-17}$

This incident is similar to that in Mark 3$^{1-6}$. The ruler of the synagogue did not like to address Jesus directly, so he addressed his criticisms to the congregation. By a *daughter of Abraham* Jesus meant a Jewess. Her affliction, some sort of spinal curvature, or perhaps just chronic weakness, was regarded, as was sickness generally, as the work of Satan. This, no less than compassion, justified instant action.

72 · The Lament for Jerusalem   Luke 13$^{31-35}$.
                                                   Matthew 23$^{37-39}$

Luke 13$^{31-33}$ belongs only to Luke. The warning in v. 31 was possibly friendly. Joanna the wife of Chuza, Herod's steward, was one of the women who ministered to Jesus, so inside information from Herod's court would easily reach him. *Fox* was a symbol not only of cunning but also of destructiveness and worthlessness. The expression *the third day* meant 'in a short time'. Jesus would be *perfected* when his work was completed. V. 33 ends in the grim comment that, since Jerusalem was the place where prophets got slain, Herod had no chance to harm Jesus.

This threat to Jesus raises a difficulty. Shortly before (Luke 9$^{51-56}$) Luke describes Jesus' visit to a hostile Samaritan village. Samaria on the west of Jordan was not in Herod's territory, but Peraea, on the east side, was. Which route to Jerusalem was Jesus taking? Three explanations are possible:

(1) Jesus attempted to take the Samaritan route, but, finding the Samaritans hostile, changed his mind and journeyed through Peraea.

(2) The journey through Peraea took place on another visit to

Jerusalem. (Jesus must have visited the holy city much more often than the Synoptic Gospels suggest. The Fourth Gospel is evidence of this.)

(3) Jesus, in no particular hurry to reach Jerusalem, was busy with evangelistic work on the way, and sometimes crossed over Jordan.

The idea of God's people finding refuge under his protective wings is frequent in the Old Testament (Deuteronomy 32^{11}, Ruth 2^{12}, Psalm 17^8). The words used by Jesus are from the Apocrypha, II Esdras 1^{30}. They are interpreted by scholars in varying ways:

(1) The words quoted were attributed to God. Jesus therefore was speaking as the Son of God, and using the words personally. *How often* refers to his previous visits (and appeals) to Jerusalem.

(2) Jesus was quoting the words of God and speaking on behalf of God. Jesus therefore was speaking as a prophet. Thus *how often* refers to God's own repeated attempts through his prophets to save his people.

(3) In Matthew this Lament comes at the end of the Woes on scribes and Pharisees. The corresponding section of Woes in Luke (11$^{37-52}$) says, *Therefore also said the wisdom of God, I will send unto them prophets and apostles; and some of them they shall kill and persecute.* It is therefore suggested that Luke's Lament has been detached from its original position in the document from which Matthew and Luke took it.

From this it is concluded that the speaker in this Lament is the Wisdom of God personified in later Jewish literature. It is pointed out that Jesus could not mean that he himself was a refugee such as could be found under God's wings. The words *Ye shall not see me* are reminiscent of references to the Wisdom of God in Jewish literature, where Wisdom is thought of as becoming hidden for a time. After wars and other troubles, Wisdom would return again as the Elect One.

The first Christians, however, Matthew and Luke included, thought of Jesus and the Wisdom of God as one and the same. They therefore would regard these words of Jesus as spoken by him in his own right as Son of God, the Wisdom of God, and the Elect One, or Messiah. (See Matthew 11$^{28-30}$ for another passage where Jesus speaks of himself as the Wisdom of God.)

Your house is left unto you desolate refers to the destruction of the Temple in A.D. 70. God would then abandon his dwelling-place, and this would mean that his presence was no longer in the midst of his people. Many prophets, including Jeremiah, had foretold this. Ezekiel, in a vision, saw the glory of God leaving, and returning to, his Temple. Josephus, the Jewish historian of the first century, writing about the actual destruction of the Temple, tells how, before its final destruction by the armies of Titus, the doors mysteriously opened, and the angel guardians were heard departing.

Blessed is he that cometh comes from Psalm 118²⁶. This was a psalm used to welcome pilgrims. It had special associations with the Feast of Tabernacles, and was used to welcome Jesus on Palm Sunday. In Matthew these words of Jesus come after 'Palm Sunday', so it is possible that Matthew here understood Jesus to be predicting his second coming (an event which the first Christians believed would coincide with the destruction of Jerusalem). In Luke, however, the words are spoken before 'Palm Sunday', and seem to predict only that. This leaves us uncertain as to their precise application.

73 · The Man with the Dropsy
Luke 14¹⁻⁶

The story is rather like that of the man with the withered hand (Mark 3¹⁻⁶) and the healing of the crippled woman (Luke 13¹⁰⁻¹⁷) (see Sections 41 and 71). The man in the story may have been either a guest or an onlooker. It was not unusual for Jesus to be invited to a meal by Pharisees, but their motives were rarely friendly.

It was possible on this occasion that Jesus told the parable about those who chose the chief seats. See Section 161 No. 13.

74 · The Storm on the Sea of Galilee
Mark 4³⁵⁻⁴¹. Luke 8²²⁻²⁵. Matthew 8¹⁸, ²³⁻²⁷

This is one of the few nature miracles, i.e. miracles not of healing. (Other nature miracles are the feeding of the five thousand and the miraculous catch of fish.) Sudden storms were one of the dangers of the lake. It lies in the northern end of the Great Rift Valley, which forms a deep ravine along which storms can rage. Storms were known to occur and end suddenly. The distance across was about five miles.

Many Jews believed that storms were caused by evil spirits. Mark reports the words of Jesus as if he were indeed addressing a storm demon, and telling it to 'be muzzled'. He tells the story to show how the power of Jesus over the elements revealed his divinity.

LUKE and MATTHEW. Luke and Matthew follow Mark, with a noticeable difference in the disciples' words to Jesus. They are much more polite than Mark: *Master, master, we perish* (Luke), and *Save, Lord; we perish* (Matthew). By the time these Gospels were written the apostles had become revered figures in the Christian community. These authors, therefore, seem to have felt the need to tone down the bluntness of Mark's report.

75 · The Gerasene Demoniac

Mark 5$^{1-20}$. Luke 8$^{26-39}$.
Matthew 8$^{28-34}$

Alternative names for the place where this miracle occurred are Gerasa, Gadara, Gergesa. The actual site is hard to identify. Because pigs are mentioned it seems likely that it was in Gentile territory, because Jews regarded pigs as 'unclean' animals.

All forms of madness were thought to be the result of demon possession. Demons, having no bodies of their own, had to inhabit the bodies of human beings or animals, in order to express themselves. Thus when a madman spoke it was really the demon speaking.

The madman lived among the rock-hewn tombs of a cemetery. His madness gave him more than normal strength. As in other miracles of exorcism mentioned by Mark, his demons recognized the identity of Jesus. It was a common belief that to know the name of a demon gave one power over it. Legion was the name of a division in the Roman army of between 3,000 and 6,000 men. The answer seems to indicate that the man was possessed by numerous demons, and was therefore a bad case of madness; but the man could have been thinking of himself as leading a legion of the dead in the cemetery where he dwelt.

According to popular belief, when the pigs were drowned the demons would be destroyed also.

This is the one occasion when Jesus told someone to speak about a miracle instead of to keep quiet. This was because there was no danger here of crowds following just to see miracles. Only once did Jesus visit that country again.

The question arises, were the pigs destroyed by the wish of Jesus? They may have been, if Jesus felt that the well-being of the man was more important than that of animals. On the other hand, on no other occasion when Jesus cast out evil spirits is there any suggestion that they found another dwelling-place, and here no actual command is recorded (see Luke 11^{24} and Matthew 12^{43}).

A possible reconstruction of events is this: The swineherds' attention was distracted by the lunatic rushing towards Jesus. Knowing the man to be dangerous, they were amazed when suddenly he became sane. The swineherds drew nearer, and the neglected pigs wandered too near the cliff edge. The swineherds noticed this, and ran to the pigs (or perhaps the lunatic startled the pigs as he was about to be healed). The frightened pigs ran over the cliff instead of inland.

The swineherds, when reporting the loss to the owners, would not say that they had been negligent, but would rather blame the healing of the lunatic. It would seem to them that the evil spirits must have found a new home in the pigs, and that all had been destroyed together. Peter who saw the miracle, and Mark, who wrote it down, would also assume, like anyone else, that the loss of the pigs was caused by the evil spirits leaving the man, and that Jesus had commanded them to do so and enter the pigs.

LUKE. Luke follows Mark.

MATTHEW. Matthew's account is a much abbreviated form of Mark's. He names the place of the miracle as Gadara, and has two madmen instead of one. This is regarded by some as an example of Matthew's tendency to make adaptations of and additions to the stories taken from Mark, so as to make them more impressive. In this Gospel only does Jesus appear to give a command to the evil spirits actually to enter the swine. Even so, his only word is *Go*, and that could mean no more than *Go out*.

76 · The Daughter of Jairus   Mark 5²¹⁻⁴³. Luke 8⁴⁰⁻⁵⁶. Matthew 9¹⁸⁻²⁶

It was the duty of a 'ruler' of a synagogue to arrange its services and administer its affairs. Jairus was possibly the chief of such rulers. The woman with the haemorrhage or *issue of blood* came to Jesus secretly because, according to the Law of Moses, her affliction made her 'unclean' (Leviticus 15).

V. 35 implies that the father's agitation had been aggravated by the delay. The *tumult* in v. 38 was designed to keep away evil spirits. Mourners were hired for the purpose. V. 41 gives the Aramaic words that Jesus spoke. V. 43 shows his thoughtfulness. The girl had been ill, and would have had nothing much to eat. Now she would be hungry. Moreover, Jesus' request would provide her excited mother with something practical to do.

Some scholars suggest that the girl had not really died, but was only in a coma. They point out that *(a)* the only mention of her death comes from the messengers who brought the news to Jairus; *(b)* Jesus himself said *the child is not dead*; and *(c)* there was no time for hired mourners to be already at the house.

Against these points the following should be observed: *(a)* Why should the messengers' word not be true? The people at the house were surely capable of recognizing death. *(b)* Jesus had not yet seen the body (see Luke) and could have been trying to reassure the father, or he was thinking of death as sleep. The first Christians thought of death in this way (John 11¹¹, Acts 7⁶⁰). So Mark could assume that Jesus was doing so. In any case the people at the house *laughed him to scorn* when they heard his words. *(c)* Very little time would be lost in getting hired mourners. The Jairus family was important; the girl's death was expected. Whether the hired mourners had arrived or not (they were probably not far away in case they were needed) there were the servants of the household and interested neighbours ready to begin wailing immediately death occurred.

LUKE. Luke follows Mark, except for a few differences. In view of the tradition that Luke was a doctor, it is interesting to note that he is much kinder to the medical profession than Mark; when he mentions that the woman had consulted many doctors, he does not add Mark's note that the woman *was nothing bettered, but rather grew worse.*

Luke also modifies the hasty and rather rude reply made by the disciples to Jesus' question, *Who is it that touched me?*

Luke mentions that it was the *border of his garment* that the woman touched. This was the ceremonial fringe or tassel as prescribed by the Law. But Luke does not give the Aramaic words spoken by Jesus to Jairus's daughter, as does Mark; and Jesus' words, *She is not dead* are spoken after he has seen the body.

MATTHEW. Matthew's account is a considerably abbreviated form of Mark. Matthew omits the mention of the ruler's name, the physicians consulted by the woman, the fact that Jesus had to stop and ask who touched him, the messengers with the news of the girl's death, the parents, Peter James and John, any words spoken by Jesus to the girl, and the request that she should be given food. *The border of his garment* which the woman touched was the ceremonial fringe or tassel prescribed by the Law.

77 · A Return Visit to Nazareth

Mark 6$^{1-6}$. Luke 4$^{16-30}$. Matthew 13$^{53-58}$

By now the fame of Jesus had spread throughout Galilee, and not least into Nazareth, *his own country*, where he had spent the greater part of his life. Jesus returned there with his disciples to engage in missionary work, but it was soon evident that he was too well known by the people of Nazareth for them to have much respect for him.

Jesus was known as *the carpenter*. Joseph had probably died some years before, and Jesus had taken over the business. People also called him *son of Mary*, which was a way of saying that he was illegitimate because a Jew was always known as the son of his father, even if the father were dead (see Section 68 and below).

LUKE. Luke places his account of Jesus' return to Nazareth at the beginning of his ministry, and immediately after the temptations. Possibly Luke wanted to show why Jesus made Capernaum instead of Nazareth the centre of his Galilean ministry. Luke's story is far more detailed than Mark's, and only he records the violent attempt to kill Jesus.

The greater part of a synagogue service consisted of a reading of the Law and the words of the prophets. These readings were followed by explanations and instructions. The passage was read standing; the exposition was given seated. Jesus was asked to read as a visiting rabbi. It was in this very same synagogue that he had first learned to read.

The words read were the words of the unknown prophet now referred to as Third Isaiah (i.e. chapters 56–66) because his writings, along with those of another unnamed prophet, the Second Isaiah (i.e. chapters 40–55) have from ancient times been included in the Old Testament with those of the great statesman prophet, Isaiah of Jerusalem. In the words read, Third Isaiah was thinking of the Servant Songs contained in Second Isaiah.

These Servant Songs considerably influenced Jesus in his role of Messiah (see Section 30). So here he made the prophet's words his own. Aware that his listeners expected him to demonstrate his right to do so, he quoted a proverb, *Physician heal thyself*. He then went on to remind them that God's favour was not confined to Jews, and gave two notable examples from history, one from I Kings 17, the other from II Kings 5. This, and the suggestion that his own mission was equally broad, aroused his audience to fury.

Jesus' escape from death is often regarded as a miracle, but it need not have been. It is possible that by the time that the precipice was reached anger had cooled, and the people remembered that, being in an occupied country, they would be answerable to the Romans for any disturbance, especially if it resulted in a death. Jesus walked away from Nazareth never to return again.

MATTHEW. Matthew's account is based on Mark's, but *Is not this the carpenter?* (Mark 6³) becomes in v. 55, *Is not this the carpenter's son?* The alteration is thought to be due to a mistaken sense of reverence felt for Jesus by some early Christians, who did not like to think that he was ever a mere workman.

Another interesting alteration comes in v. 58, where Mark's *could not* becomes *did not*, so that there should be no suggestion that Jesus lacked the power to perform miracles (cf. Section 34, Matthew 8¹⁶, and Mark 1³⁴).

Mission Tours

78 · The Gospel of the Kingdom   Matthew 9^{35–38}

The kingdom of God was the theme that dominated the teaching of Jesus. The kingdom itself came with Jesus, and his healing of *all manner of disease and all manner of sickness* was a visible sign that the work of evil was being overthrown by the stronger power of God. All the people waiting to be gathered into the kingdom were like sheep without a shepherd, and like a harvest waiting to be reaped (see Section 158).

79 · The Twelve go on a Mission Tour

Mark 6^{7–15, 30}.
Luke 9^{1–10}.
Matthew 10^{1, 5–15}

The apostles went in pairs for company. Their healing powers presumably were limited to the duration of the tour. The Twelve were not to be over-burdened with goods, but were to take only staff and sandals. They were to rely on people's generosity for their needs, but were not to go as beggars with a collecting wallet. Jews regarded hospitality to strangers at any time of day or night as a very important duty. (Genesis 18 tells how Abraham once entertained three strangers who were angels in disguise.) To offer hospitality to a holy man or preacher was an honour (II Kings 4⁸).

To *shake off the dust* meant, 'We want nothing more to do with you; even the dust you can take back!' Jews were very particular about 'shaking off the dust' if they had been in Gentile lands. The apostles were not to linger where they were not wanted. Oil was frequently used in the East to help healing, but anointing the sick with oil became a Christian practice for spiritual rather than medical healing.

This preaching and healing tour extended the sphere of Jesus' work in Galilee, and called attention to it. People spoke of him as a prophet, or as one of the Old Testament prophets, such as Elijah, who had returned.

King Herod's guilty conscience suggested that Jesus was perhaps John the Baptist come back to trouble him further.

LUKE. Luke's account is based on Mark's, but he does not mention that the Twelve went two by two, and that the sick were anointed. According to him the disciples were forbidden to take even a staff, and other people said that Jesus was perhaps John the Baptist. Herod did not, though he wondered who Jesus was.

MATTHEW. Matthew does not mention that the Twelve went two by two, as does Mark, but he does list the names of the Twelve at this point (see Section 43). In vv. 5 and 9 Matthew adds to the commands recorded by Mark one about confining the mission to Jews, and one forbidding shoes as well as staff.

Jesus completes his instructions with a warning that in the day of judgement Sodom and Gomorrah (cities mentioned in Genesis 19 and destroyed because of their wickedness) would be dealt with more leniently than a city that rejected the message of the kingdom.

Vv. 16–42 are instructions given by Jesus on a later occasion, and are about the great mission of the early Church in spreading the Christian Faith in the world (see Section 81). The mission of the Twelve was comparatively a small affair in Galilee.

80 · The Mission of the Seventy   Luke 10$^{1-20}$

This mission, mentioned only by Luke, is similar in a number of ways to the mission of the Twelve in Luke 9$^{1-6}$ (and Mark 6$^{7-13}$). Because of this some scholars think that the mission of the Seventy is but another version of the mission of the Twelve. But why should Luke put both into one Gospel? One reason might be that, as it is characteristic of Matthew to portray Jesus as the Jewish Messiah, so it is characteristic of Luke to show Jesus as the world's Saviour.

Seventy or seventy-two was regarded as the number of the nations of the world. Some manuscripts of Luke do indeed have seventy-two as sent on the mission. In the light of this, Luke's account of the mission of the Twelve would represent the preaching of the Gospel to the Jews (by representatives of the twelve tribes) and the mission of the Seventy, or Seventy-two, would represent the preaching of the Gospel to the world (by representatives of the number of the nations).

Another suggestion is that, as in English numbering the figures 1 and 2 could easily become in copying 7 and 2, so the Greek signs for 12 and 72 could be confused. Then by the time that Luke selected the material for his Gospel one manuscript might read 12 and another 72, thus giving the appearance of two separate tours.

It is possible, of course, that Jesus did send his disciples on two separate missions, the second one being more extensive than the first, and at a date when the apostles were retained more in his company.

81 · The Mission Charge   Matthew 10$^{16-42}$. Luke 12$^{1-12,\ 49-53}$

The Synoptic Gospels describe how Jesus sent the Twelve upon a mission tour (Mark 6$^{7-15}$, Luke 9$^{1-10}$, Matthew 10$^{1,\ 5-15}$) and Luke mentions a tour undertaken by seventy disciples (Luke 10$^{1-24}$). In each instance the instructions to the missionaries are recorded.

Matthew, however, adds a further mission charge, which scholars believe belongs to some instructions given by Jesus at a much later date, since the Twelve and the Seventy on their Galilean tour were not in danger of the violent persecution described in this passage. Matthew seems to have collected together an anthology of Jesus' teaching from several sources. In particular the passage has much in common with Jesus' apocalyptic teaching on the Mount of Olives (cf. Mark 13, Luke 21$^{5-38}$, Matthew 24), and also with the warnings given after Peter's confession, (cf. Mark 8$^{34-38}$, Luke 9$^{23-27}$, Matthew 16$^{24-28}$, see Sections 94 and 124).

Luke presents the words of Jesus not as a mission charge, but rather as words of encouragement to the Twelve after warning them to beware of the evil influences of the Pharisees. Vv. 2–12 in Luke correspond to Matthew 10$^{19-20,\ 25-33}$.

In both Gospels appear the need to fear Satan more than those who could kill the body, and the assurance of God's care. Both make it clear that the impact of the religion of Jesus upon the world will be such that division rather than unity will result. In Luke 12^{49} Jesus is possibly thinking that the impact of his coming is already causing conflict.

In Luke 12^{50} Jesus uses the word *baptism* as a symbol of suffering (cf. Mark 10$^{38-40}$). He seems to be thinking of his coming death, and wishing that it were over. It may be that he felt that his work of bringing in the kingdom was being frustrated or limited until his death had taken place.

82 · The Galilean Cities Condemned   Luke 10$^{13-16,\ 21-24}$. Matthew 11$^{20-30}$

LUKE. The Woes recorded here are not to be found in the other mission accounts. It seems that, although people had flocked to Jesus during his ministry in Galilee, he was disappointed at their response. So, when his work in Galilee was almost ended, Jesus condemned the cities around the lake.

Heathen cities like Tyre and Sidon, inhabited by Gentiles, he considered, would have made a more ready response. They therefore would have a better chance in the day of judgement because in their day they knew no better. Capernaum of all places, honoured because Jesus made it his headquarters and the centre of his work, would receive the sternest judgement of all, because its opportunity had been the greatest (cf. vv. 13–16 with Luke 11²⁹⁻³² and the demand for a sign in Section 67).

V. 18 could refer to some pre-cosmic happening, but it could mean only that the defeat of evil was already certain, as the work of the kingdom went ahead. To *tread on serpents and scorpions* was a metaphor for the triumph of good over evil.

LUKE and MATTHEW. The *babes* in Luke 10²¹ and Matthew 11²⁵ were the simple folk in contrast with the religious leaders.

Luke 10²⁴ and Matthew 11²⁷ are important because they show how conscious was Jesus of a close and unique relationship with God. Jesus alone could make God known to men because Jesus alone really knew the Father and was known by him. These verses are more like much of the contents of the Fourth Gospel than of the synoptic three.

The things longed for in Luke 10²⁴ were the coming of the kingdom.

MATTHEW. Matthew, instead of mentioning that Jesus told the Twelve that they were fortunate to see the coming of the kingdom, as does Luke, adds some significant verses of his own in 11²⁸⁻³⁰. These words are very similar to some found in the apocryphal book Ecclesiasticus (6²⁴⁻²⁸, 24¹⁹⁻²¹, 51²³⁻²⁷). This, with the Old Testament books, Job, Proverbs, Ecclesiastes, belongs to the class of writing known as Wisdom Literature, so called because it is about the Divine Wisdom, and how desirable it is for human beings to seek it.

By the time Ecclesiasticus was written (not before 200 B.C.) people had thought so much about God's Wisdom that they often spoke of it as though it were a person. In the Wisdom Literature, therefore, it is not unusual to find the Wisdom of God (or the Word of God, which is a similar idea) speaking to men, and inviting them to *Come unto me*.

These verses in Matthew, showing Jesus speaking as the Divine Wisdom, and bidding men *learn of me*, had special importance for the first Christians, since they regarded Jesus as the Divine Wisdom (or Word) revealed to men in human form (cf. John 1¹⁴).

70

83 · Martha and Mary   Luke 10³⁸⁻⁴²

The *certain village* is not named in the Synoptic Gospels, but the Fourth Gospel says that it was Bethany, and that the sisters lived there with their brother Lazarus, whom Jesus raised from the dead (John 11). Bethany, however, is very close to Jerusalem (it was when approaching Bethany that Jesus sent his disciples for an ass on which to ride into the city) and at this point in Luke's account Jesus is still a long way off.

A likely explanation is either that the story has got displaced in Luke's narrative, and should have been put later, or that this incident happened upon some other visit to Jerusalem, of which the Fourth Gospel makes mention but not the Synoptists.

In v. 42 Jesus tells Martha that she is anxious about preparing a lot of things when one would do. In a play upon words, he says that in effect Mary has chosen the best portion of all. (The Greek word for 'part' means also a 'portion' of food.)

84 · The Death of John the Baptist   Mark 6¹⁴⁻²⁹. Luke 9⁷⁻⁹. Matthew 14¹⁻¹²

This story is one that has probably gained much in colour from its repetition by the common people, who honoured John as a prophet and hated Herod Antipas.

Antipas had two half-brothers; one, known as Herod, lived as a private gentleman at Rome; the other, known as Philip, was tetrarch of Ituraea and Trachonitis (Luke 3¹). The husband of Herodias was Herod in Rome. Salome was their daughter. She became eventually the wife of Philip. It has been thought that Herod in Rome was also called Philip, in which case Mark is right in giving this name to Herodias's husband; but some think that in this Mark may have confused the first husband of Herodias with the husband of Salome.

Antipas, on a visit to Herod in Rome, persuaded Herodias to divorce her husband and marry him, while he divorced his own wife (a daughter of King Aretas, mentioned in II Corinthians 11³²) to marry her. John the Baptist earned the displeasure of Herod Antipas, and the hatred of Herodias, for denouncing this second marriage as against Jewish Law (Leviticus 18¹⁶). Herodias would have had John put to death immediately, but Herod, like everyone else, regarded him as a holy man, and feared to kill him.

LUKE. Luke mentions here only that Herod beheaded John, because Luke has already introduced the matter in 3¹⁸⁻²⁰.

MATTHEW. Matthew's account is a slightly abbreviated form of Mark.

85 · The Feeding of the Five Thousand

Mark 6³¹⁻⁴⁴. Luke 9¹⁰⁻¹⁷. Matthew 14¹³⁻²¹ (John 6¹⁻¹⁴)

This is one of the nature miracles, and the only one recorded in all four Gospels. It was obviously a very significant miracle for the early Christians. The telling of it is probably coloured by thoughts from the Christian Communion Service. The site is uncertain. Possibly it was on some grassy slopes near Bethsaida or Capernaum. The baskets could have come from the fishing boat in which Jesus sailed.

Scholars hold varying views about the miracle. The main adverse criticisms are as follows:

(1) Some scholars think that this was only a token meal, and that people received only a fragment of food. But *(a)* without a miracle five loaves and two fish would not have been sufficient to provide even this; *(b)* the Gospels say, *they did all eat, and were filled*; *(c)* there were left twelve basketsful of fragments, which was more food than Jesus had to begin with.

(2) Some people say that the people just shared food that they had brought with them. (People in the East do not travel far without taking food.) And the first Christians turned the incident into a miracle, because they were influenced by a story about Elisha (II Kings 4⁴²⁻⁴⁴). But *(a)* the people started off in a hurry; *(b)* they had been with Jesus for some time, and any food with them had probably been eaten already. In any case there would surely not be more than was needed, to the extent of twelve basketsful; *(c)* a picnic would scarcely have given the impression of being a miracle. Plenty of people saw it, and four evangelists write about it. They lived nearer the time of the incident than we do.

(3) The number of people was exaggerated. But even fifty people would need more than five loaves and two fish to feed them sufficiently.

(4) Jesus' action was out of accord with his resolution in the wilderness not to be diverted into founding an earthly welfare state. But *(a)* according to the Fourth Gospel, although people were so moved by this miracle that they wanted to make him king, Jesus evaded them (John 6¹⁵); *(b)* Jesus fed the people on this occasion because he was sorry for them, which was not the same as doing this sort of thing regularly; *(c)* by performing the miracle Jesus demonstrated the generosity of God. (The first Christians were probably right when they regarded this miracle, when Jesus fed people physically, as a preparation

for the time when he would feed them spiritually. In the Fourth Gospel Jesus' teaching about the Bread of Life follows shortly afterwards.)

86 · Jesus Walks on the Water   Mark 6[45-56]. Matthew 14[22-36]

Jesus sent the Twelve away by boat possibly because the people wanted to make him king (John 6[15]) and Jesus feared that the Twelve might encourage them. V. 52 suggests that the Twelve could not understand why Jesus had missed the opportunity, or so they thought, of being made a king. V. 48 suggests that Jesus from some high vantage-point could see his disciples in danger well out on the water. The time was between 3 a.m. and 6 a.m.

It is, of course, perfectly possible that this miracle happened just as the Gospel says, remembering who Jesus is, but the following alternative suggestions have been made:

(1) The Greek phrase translated *walking on the sea* could be translated 'walking by the sea'. Jesus therefore walked along the shore while the boat kept near to the land for safety. In the moonlight Jesus looked as though he were on the water. The phrase in v. 48, *would have passed by them* supports this theory, as also does Peter's attempt (in Matthew) to go to meet Jesus.

(2) The incident is the same as that in John 21. Peter's going from the boat (in Matthew) is repeated in John.

(3) The story is symbolic. The boat containing the Twelve represents the Church tossed about by the storms of persecution. When all is dark, and the coming of Jesus seems distant, he comes, at daybreak, to succour his suffering Church, and the storm ceases. (It had been during the morning watch that God had come to the aid of his people as they crossed the Red Sea. Exodus 14[24].) The story would help and inspire Christians in Rome suffering persecution by Nero at the time when Mark's Gospel was written.

(4) The story is that of the stilling of the storm (Mark 4[35-41]) re-told.

MATTHEW. Matthew takes his account from Mark, except for the important addition concerning Peter. Possibly Matthew was anxious to show reason for the great prominence of Peter in the early Church.

87 · Jewish Ceremonial Cleansing   Mark 7[1-23]. Matthew 15[1-20]

In vv. 1–8 Mark gives a lot of detailed information about Jewish ceremonial washings, because he is writing for Gentile Christians who will not be familiar with such rules.

73

The criticism of Jesus and the Twelve by the scribes and Pharisees had nothing to do with hygienic washing. Their complaint was that he and the apostles did not observe the regulations about ceremonial washing after being in contact with Gentiles. Jews frequently had to do business with Gentiles, or purchase cups and pots that had been in contact with Gentiles.

Pharisees were particularly scrupulous about this ceremonial washing. They washed the hands right up to the elbow (R.V. margin) before *eating bread*, i.e. having a meal. By so doing their hands were sanctified or consecrated, as opposed to being *defiled*, or common, or profane.

The religious reason behind all this ceremonial washing was a long out-dated superstition that certain objects were inhabited by spirits, and that contact with them made a person polluted, or unclean, until the infection had been washed away. In instances of contact with Gentiles, with Jews who did not keep the Law, and with the dead, the primitive idea of uncleanness still survived.

The washings were regulated not by the Law of Moses but by the *traditions* of the scribes and elders, which, being by them considered to be of equal importance with the Law, could in some cases actually reverse that Law. In vv. 9–13 Jesus gave an example. Despite the Fifth Commandment, a Jew could get out of the responsibility to support his parents by offering his money as a gift (*corban*, in Aramaic) to the Temple. He could not then touch it in order to help his parents. It had become dedicated.

'By corban' was also an oath whereby a person swore by the gift or sacrifice on the Temple altar. If a Jew used such an oath, however thoughtlessly, when refusing to help his parents, the oath could not be broken. Thus, said Jesus, the Law of God could not be kept because the traditions over-ruled it. Not all rabbis would have upheld such evasion. Many would have agreed with Jesus. The fact remained, however, that the traditions made such a thing possible.

Vv. 14–23 are a return to the subject of ceremonial washing. Jesus said that it was not meat (unclean because it was eaten with unclean hands) going into a man that could defile him. The wickedness coming from within the heart of a man was the cause of real religious uncleanness.

The whole of this section of Mark would have been of great interest to his readers. They were themselves Gentiles, and they knew well the controversy that had raged between Jewish Christians and Gentile converts. Some of the original Christians had said that Gentiles must become as it were Jews, and keep the Jewish Law, before being baptized as Christians. Others, particularly St. Paul, had said that Gentiles needed only to be baptized. Along with this went the problem of Jewish Christians eating with Gentile Christians, when the former felt bound by laws regarding 'clean' and 'unclean' meats.

By the time that Mark wrote his Gospel these controversies were, for the most part, settled, but hostility from Jews who were not Christians continued, and Jesus' attitude towards the Law and the traditions would be read with interest.

MATTHEW. Matthew mainly follows Mark, but he omits Mark's details about ceremonial washings, and adds Peter's name to the request by the disciples that Jesus should explain his meaning further.

88 · Jesus Heals a Gentile Woman's Daughter

Mark 7$^{24-30}$.
Matthew 15$^{21-31}$

It is very appropriate that the passage dealing with Jesus' attitude towards contact with Gentiles should be followed, in Mark and Matthew by a story showing him healing the daughter of a Gentile woman. Tyre and Sidon were two famous seaports of Phoenicia. The house entered was therefore a Gentile one.

The dialogue given in vv. 27–29 was evidently light-hearted and humorous. The mention of *dogs* and *crumbs* arose probably because Jesus was having a meal when the woman arrived, and the pet dogs were getting pieces thrown down from the table. As well as pet dogs, there were in Palestine wild dogs, and Jews often referred to Gentiles as such dogs. In this conversation, when speaking about the Gentiles, Jesus referred more kindly to pet dogs. The *children* were the Jews.

Jesus was saying as gently as possible that his work at the moment was properly among Jews. The woman was asking him to give what was theirs to Gentiles, to give, as it were, the children's bread to the dogs. The woman's reply was that, even while waiting their turn, the dogs did get something.

In the three short years of his public ministry Jesus obviously had to concentrate his efforts upon being the Messiah of the Jews. After the resurrection and ascension, however, the Christian Faith was offered to the Gentiles, and the Gentiles received it more readily than did Jews. By that time the *children* had had their turn, and the *dogs* were indeed getting theirs. Some of Jesus' parables are about the Gentiles having their chance (see Sections 117, 160 Nos. 8 and 9).

This miracle is an example of Jesus' healing at a distance, and of his association with Gentiles (see Section 62).

MATTHEW. Matthew, who was writing his Gospel for Jewish Christians, gives a much more Jewish slant upon the story than does Mark. Thus:

(1) Jesus did not go outside Jewish territory: the Gentile woman *came out from those borders* into Jewish territory. There is no mention therefore of Jesus entering the house of a Gentile.

(2) Matthew calls the woman *Canaanitish* instead of Syro-Phoenician. His description is thus somewhat more contemptuous. In the early days of Israel's history the Jewish religion suffered more contamination from Canaanite religion than from any other source. The great prophets fought Canaanite influence, and tried to keep the Jews loyal to God. In later years, when the danger was past, Jews still regarded Canaanite Gentiles as more unclean than others.

(3) When the woman appeals to Jesus, Matthew adds the very Jewish title for the Messiah, i.e. Son of David. He also adds to Jesus' reply, *I was not sent but unto the lost sheep of . . . Israel.*

(4) A fourth difference from Mark is the detail that Jesus ignored the woman until the disciples begged him to *send her away.*

89 · Healing in Decapolis   Mark 7³¹⁻³⁷

Decapolis (Greek for Ten Cities) was the district south of the Sea of Galilee, on the east side of Jordan. It was here that the Gerasene demoniac went to tell people about his cure.

The man in this story was deaf and almost dumb. Jesus took him aside to avoid sightseers. Jesus rarely used any special outward action when performing a miracle. On this occasion he touched the man's ears, and used saliva on his tongue. According to ancient belief saliva had healing properties. Such a cure is attributed to the Emperor Vespasian (see Section 92).

Jesus did not need to use these special signs, but they probably helped the faith of the man being healed. Being deaf he would be unable to hear any explanation as to why a stranger was leading him away. When he saw Jesus' actions, he would understand that he was to be healed. Mark carefully preserves the actual Aramaic word that Jesus spoke. This time Jesus asked the man to keep quiet about the cure, unlike the Gerasene demoniac who was asked to talk about his.

The miracle reminded people of how Isaiah had said of the Messianic Age, *The eyes of the blind shall be opened, and the ears of the deaf shall be unstopped* (Isaiah 35⁵).

90 · The Feeding of the Four Thousand   Mark 8[1-10]. Matthew 15[29-39]

This account of the feeding of the four thousand is so similar to that of the five thousand that most scholars think it to be a duplicate account, with slight variations as to the number of loaves, fish, and baskets left over. Both accounts, moreover, are followed by a voyage on the lake and a dispute with Pharisees.

Possibly Mark got the one account from Peter, who was very much at the centre of things on the occasion of the feeding of the five thousand, and another account from someone who had been one of the crowd, and who would not be so likely to know exactly how many loaves and fish Jesus used, or how many baskets of crumbs remained. By the time that Mark wrote his Gospel Peter was dead, and Mark could not ask him whether the miracle happened once or twice. Mark therefore included both accounts.

There is, of course, the obvious possibility that Jesus did perform such a miracle on two (or even more) occasions. If, however, the feeding of the four thousand was a second occasion, why were the disciples still at a loss as to what could be done? It would have to be a very long time after the feeding of the five thousand for them to forget so completely.

Some scholars suggest that the two accounts are meant to be symbolic. The feeding of the five thousand took place in Galilee, and represents the feeding of the Jews; the feeding of the four thousand took place in Decapolis, and represents the feeding by Jesus of the Gentiles. Further symbolism, though probably exaggerated, is sometimes seen in the twelve basketsful and the seven basketsful – respectively the twelve apostles and the seven deacons mentioned in Acts 6.

No one knows where Dalmanutha was.

MATTHEW. Matthew takes his account from Mark. He mentions a place called Magadan instead of Dalmanutha. No one knows where either place was.

91 · The Leaven of the Pharisees   Mark 8[14-21]. Luke 12[1]. Matthew 16[5-12]

Leaven is any substance that causes dough to rise in baking. (The kind most familiar to us is yeast.) Leaven was a very apt illustration of the way in which an influence, good or bad, can spread. Rabbis often used it for evil influence. Yeast in a bowl of flour spreads quietly and imperceptibly, but with very obvious results. In the parable of The Leaven

77

(Matthew 13³³) Jesus used it to illustrate the spread of the kingdom; here it seems he uses it to illustrate the bad influence of the Pharisees and Herodians, who were conspiring together against him (cf. Mark 3⁶ and 12¹³).

This is one of the occasions when Mark shows how slow the disciples were to understand Jesus and have faith in him. His answer to them in v. 18 is very similar to the words of God to Isaiah during his vision in the Temple (Isaiah 6¹⁰). Since Jesus had recently fed a whole multitude, there was no reason why the disciples should be anxious. In vv. 19 and 20 Mark mentions two miracles because he has written about two incidents.

LUKE. The warning in Luke 12¹ is in a different context, and given on a different occasion, from that mentioned by Mark and Matthew.

MATTHEW. Matthew's account is similar to Mark's, except that Matthew mentions *the leaven of the Pharisees and Sadducees* instead of the leaven of Pharisees and Herod (as in Mark) and further explains that the *leaven* is their teaching. Jesus had just been engaged in argument with these two important Jewish sects.

Scholars point out that the author, a member of a Jewish-Christian community, uses these words of Jesus to warn his readers against those who wished to keep Christianity merely as a Jewish sect. In the early days of the Church there had been much controversy about the admission of Gentiles into it (Acts 15). Very strict Jews who became Christians wanted to keep Christianity Jewish. In this record of the warning by Jesus, the Pharisees and Sadducees represent the strict Jews.

92 · A Blind Man at Bethsaida   Mark 8²²⁻²⁶ (Matthew 9²⁷⁻³¹)

This incident, and the healing of the deaf and dumb man in Decapolis (Section 89) are miracles found only in Mark. The details of both stories are similar, and saliva is used as an outward indication of healing. The blind man's cure was not instantaneous.

MATTHEW 9²⁷⁻³¹. This miracle recorded by Matthew is similar to that in Mark. It is possible that Matthew had Mark's story in mind and combined his own with it. Thus the one man healed in Mark becomes the two men healed in Matthew. It is characteristic of Matthew to make one story do for two incidents. Compare this with Matthew 20²⁹⁻³⁴, where it appears that Matthew made a similar combination with Mark's story of blind Bartimaeus.

Caesarea Philippi and After

93 · Peter's Confession of Faith

Mark 8²⁷⁻³⁰. Luke 9¹⁸⁻²¹.
Matthew 16¹³⁻²⁰

Caesarea Philippi, a town rebuilt by the tetrarch Philip in honour of the Emperor, Caesar Augustus, lay twenty-four miles north of the Sea of Galilee, and in the foothills of Mount Hermon. Jesus went there with the Twelve.

It is noticeable that Jesus had been spending more and more time on the outskirts of Galilee and even beyond. Was this because the conspiring between the Pharisees and Herodians, the religious and civil authorities, made things increasingly dangerous for him?

While in the wilderness after his baptism, Jesus had resolved to be a different sort of Messiah from the one expected by the majority of people (see Section 30). According to the Synoptic Gospels Jesus kept secret the fact that he was the Messiah, except for a few hints for those who were specially discerning. It would have been taking too great a risk if, at the start of his ministry, he had openly announced that he was the promised Messiah, for nobody would have stopped to consider what sort of Messiah he might be. His appearance would have been a signal for revolt against Roman rule. Most people were longing for such a signal.

Meanwhile Jesus wondered about the Twelve. Had they formed any definite opinions about him? He felt that he must ask them. The incident came about half-way through Jesus' public ministry and was a very definite turning-point. The Galilean ministry was almost finished, and the journey to Jerusalem to possible death about to begin. Jesus commenced speaking to the Twelve about this. From now onward he performed fewer miracles, and spent more time in teaching. He used more frequently the phrase *Son of man*. Especially did he do so when speaking of his coming death or his coming glory (see Section 163).

LUKE. Luke's account is very similar to Mark's, but he says that Jesus was at prayer just before putting the important question to the Twelve.

79

MATTHEW. Matthew makes numerous additions to Mark, especially in vv. 17–19. He adds the name of Jeremiah to the prophets suggested. This name might well be mentioned, because Jeremiah had suffered much at the hands of the very people whom he tried to help. Indeed, apart from Jesus, Jeremiah came nearer than anyone to fufilling the Suffering Servant ideal.

Notice that in v. 16 Matthew adds to Peter's reply the words, *the Son of the living God.* Matthew also shows in v. 17 that Jesus rejoiced because of Peter's answer: it was a relief to know that the Twelve realized his true identity.

V. 18, containing the words of Jesus' reply to Peter, and the pun upon his name, is one of the most controversial in the whole New Testament.

(1) Did Jesus mean that Peter was the *rock* upon which the Church would be built? It is difficult to say, and rather depends upon the language used. Our earliest account of the words is in Greek, a language with masculine, feminine, and neuter genders (like Latin). Thus Peter, a man's name, appears in the masculine form, Petros, but the second *rock* appears in the feminine form, petra. If the second *rock* referred back to Peter, one would expect that too to be in the masculine form.

Jesus, however, did not speak these words in Greek, but in either Hebrew or Aramaic. If he spoke in Hebrew, the same distinctions of gender would apply. On the other hand, if he spoke in Aramaic, which (like English) makes no such distinction, he could very well have meant Peter when he said *upon this rock.* The mystery is, does the Greek faithfully record Jesus' meaning? No one really knows. But Peter did become a very prominent figure in the early Church, and, if any one of the Twelve could be singled out as its foundation or leader, Peter was definitely the one.

(2) Or was the *rock* upon which the Church was to be built not Peter, but the truth about Jesus that Peter had just expressed? This would make Jesus himself to be the rock.

St. Paul wrote, *Other foundation can no man lay than that which is laid, which is Jesus Christ* (I Corinthians 3[11]). In Mark 12[10, 11] Jesus quoted the words from Psalm 118[22, 23], *The stone which the builders rejected, the same was made the head of the corner* (see Section 117). Originally *the stone* described Israel, first rejected, and then raised to honour. It is thought probable that in the time of Jesus *the stone* had come to mean the Messiah. Whether this was so or not, Jesus applied the words to himself, and the first Christians did so also (e.g. Acts 4[11]). Furthermore, the first Christians were fond of picturing the Church as a building made up of living stones.

(3) A third suggestion is that Jesus never spoke the words at all. They are not mentioned in any other Gospel. Mark's Gospel, being mainly

Peter's, makes no mention of them. But then this Gospel omits other things to Peter's credit.

Of these three interpretations the first two are the most likely, and have most to be said in their favour. In view of what Jesus went on to say to Peter, scholars tend to regard the first as more likely than the second. It is certainly very probable that this was the occasion upon which Simon was given the name Peter.

It is also suggested that vv. 18 and 19 were more likely spoken after the resurrection, since Jesus speaks so precisely about founding a Church, but the precision of the statement could well be the result of its late reporting. A feature characteristic of Matthew's Gospel is the grouping together of appropriate sayings. The phrase *gates of Hades* means death. So even death has no power over the Church of Christ, i.e. his followers.

Because of the saying in v. 19 about *the keys of the kingdom of heaven*, crossed keys have become a special symbol for Peter in Christian art. The saying has also given rise to the popular idea of Peter as the door-keeper of Heaven. In the time of Jesus, however, a person entrusted with the keys of a household was no mere door-keeper, but rather the steward or controller, privileged to have access to any part of it. (See Isaiah 22^{22}, where the king's steward Shebna is deposed in favour of Eliakim, and compare Revelation 3^7 where Jesus *hath the key of David*.) It would seem that Peter's position was to be one of rule and authority in the Church.

Closely connected with the power conveyed by *the keys* is the power *to bind* and *to loose*. These were legal terms used by scribes and rabbis when interpreting the Law. *To bind* meant that something was forbidden by the Law, and *to loose* meant that it was allowed. So Peter was given authority to interpret Christian Law. This same power was given to all the Twelve in Matthew 18^{18}. By the time this Gospel was written these words meant particularly the power to excommunicate, and to reconcile, members of the early Christian Church.

94 · The First Prediction of the Passion

Mark 8^{31}–9^1.
Luke 9$^{22–27}$.
Matthew 16$^{21–28}$

As soon as the Twelve had recognized Jesus as the Messiah he began to shatter any high hopes that they might have about his future and theirs: he was indeed the Messiah, but his way was the way of the Suffering Servant. But what seemed inevitable to Jesus seemed impossible to the Twelve. Peter's words of protest were a repetition of the temptations in the wilderness.

Vv. 34–38 were probably spoken by Jesus on some other occasion. Mark mentions *the multitude* to whom he spoke, but at Caesarea Philippi Jesus was alone with the Twelve. The teaching about Christian discipleship, however, is appropriate where Mark puts it. Jesus, after predicting his own suffering and death, warned his followers to expect the same sort of future for themselves. Vv. 35–37 contain what appears to be a paradox: Jesus, of course, was speaking about life in this world and eternal life.

Having just used the title *Son of man* when speaking of his coming suffering, Jesus next used it to speak of his coming glory.

In Mark 9¹ Jesus said that some of those listening to him *shall in no wise taste of death, till they see the kingdom of God come with power*. The first Christians were quite sure that Jesus would come again in their own lifetime. The New Testament writings give ample evidence of this hope. Jesus himself at times gave this impression (e.g. 13²⁴⁻³⁷).

The first Christians did not live to see the second coming of Jesus, but they did see the coming of the kingdom of God in the Church wherever the Christian message was received. The kingdom of God came *with power* at Pentecost (Acts 2), and spread rapidly. There were Christians even in the Emperor's household before Paul arrived in Rome (Philippians 4²²). In the writings about the second coming, the near future and the distant future are at times scarcely distinguishable (see Section 124).

LUKE. Luke's account follows closely that of Mark, but he does not mention Peter's protest, nor Jesus' reply.

MATTHEW. Matthew's account follows closely that of Mark, except that Matthew adds the actual words of Peter's protest.

95 · The Transfiguration   Mark 9²⁻¹³. Luke 9²⁸⁻³⁶.
                             Matthew 17¹⁻¹³

Tradition says that the mountain was Mount Tabor, but many people now think that Mount Hermon, fourteen miles north of Caesarea Philippi, was a more likely place. For a short time the apostles saw their Messiah in his heavenly glory: his real identity broke through his human disguise. Moses represented the Jewish Law, and Elijah the prophets. Neither, so tradition said, had experienced human death.

Tabernacles, or shelters, are made by Jews from boughs of trees and bushes. Pilgrims to Jerusalem for the Feast of Tabernacles camped out on the hillsides in such booths. It was meant to remind them of the time when, in the Wilderness of Sinai, their ancestors had no fixed home and dwelt in tents. Since Jesus at times had no fixed home, the Twelve would often have made such shelters.

The over-shadowing cloud was no ordinary cloud, but the cloud of glory that surrounds God, and indicates his being present. This special cloud is often referred to by its Hebrew name, Shekinah. It led the Hebrews out of Egypt (Exodus 13²²). It covered Mount Sinai when Moses went up there to be with God (Exodus 24¹⁵⁻¹⁶). The same cloud *covered the tent of meeting* (Exodus 40³⁴). In the New Testament it is mentioned in connection with the ascension (Acts 1⁹).

Just as, at his baptism, the voice of God was heard speaking to Jesus, so now it was heard again, speaking similar words. And again the words echoed the first Servant Song (Isaiah 42¹). They echoed also the promise that God would send another prophet like Moses, and *unto him ye shall hearken* (Deuteronomy 18¹⁵⁻¹⁶).

What was the purpose of this vision? Numerous suggestions have been made. Thus:

(1) The transfiguration was a sequel to Peter's confession of faith at Caesarea Philippi. The transfiguration would help strengthen that faith for the three leading apostles.

(2) The transfiguration helped to reassure Jesus himself. God had spoken to him at his baptism, and had indicated the way of the Suffering Servant that he should take. Now, as Jesus is about to set out on the journey to the cross, the voice again gives divine approval to his action. Moses and Elijah appear, to indicate that his coming death will fulfil the Law and the prophets. (Luke says that they spoke to Jesus about his coming death.)

(3) The transfiguration of Jesus is reminiscent of the transfiguration of Moses described in Exodus 34²⁹⁻³⁵. When Moses came down from Mount Sinai *the skin of his face shone; and they were afraid to come nigh him*. St. Paul connected both incidents when he wrote a letter to Corinth (II Corinthians 3⁷⁻¹⁸). Elijah also spent time in communion with God on Mount Sinai (or Horeb). To him God spoke *in a still small voice* (I Kings 19¹²). So Moses and Elijah appear with Jesus to indicate that, great though they were, they were but pointing the way to the Messiah. According to Jewish belief both Moses and Elijah would appear before the Messiah's coming.

As they came down from the mountain, Jesus told Peter, James and John, to say nothing about their experience until *the Son of man should have risen from the dead*. (Some scholars think that the transfiguration was really a resurrection appearance recorded in the Gospels out of place.) Jesus' words about *rising again* puzzled the apostles. They had asked Jesus about Elijah's expected reappearance: they had just seen him, but what about his open reappearance to Israel? Jesus replied that

Elijah had come already (in the person of John the Baptist), and that, as John had suffered martyrdom, so the Son of man would suffer. His death was written in Scripture. Jesus was thinking of the Fourth of the Servant Songs (Isaiah 52^{13}–53^{12}).

Many scholars regard the second half of v. 12 as a question put by the apostles. (It so appears in the New English Bible.) Jesus had warned them that as the Messiah he would suffer, so they ask, *How is it written of the Son of man that he should suffer . . .?* Certainly the Scriptures did not say that the Son of man would suffer. The Servant Songs, however, indicated that the Servant would suffer. Jesus combined together the idea of the Son of man and the Suffering Servant (see Section 163).

LUKE. Luke says that this incident took place *after eight days*. He does not use the word 'transfigured' as do Mark and Matthew. This was because Luke was writing for Gentile Christians, and the word *transfigured* would suggest to Greeks and Romans the many myths and legends about heathen gods in which they changed their shape and appearance. Luke did not want the vision of Jesus in heavenly glory to be regarded as a similar story. Another detail added by Luke is that the apostles had the vision of Jesus in glory when Jesus was at prayer. Luke's interest in prayer is another characteristic of his Gospel.

Only Luke says that Moses and Elijah spoke to Jesus about his coming death. The word *decease* is really 'exodus' or 'departure'. Luke was possibly comparing the great Exodus from Egypt at Passover time, led by Moses, with the 'exodus' or 'deliverance' from the even greater bondage of sin, brought about by Jesus' sacrifice of himself on the cross, also at Passover time.

In v. 33 Luke says of Moses and Elijah, *as they were parting from him.* The figures of Moses and Elijah began to fade as though to indicate that Jesus had superseded them.

MATTHEW. Matthew's account follows closely that of Mark. His description of the transfigured Jesus is different in detail, and the voice from heaven uses all the words previously used at the baptism, plus the command, *Hear ye him.*

96 · The Healing of an Epileptic Boy

Mark 9^{14-29}.
Luke 9^{37-43}.
Matthew 17^{14-21}

This was not the apostles' first attempt at healing, for when Jesus had sent them on a mission tour he had given them power to heal (Mark 6^{13}). The epilepsy was attributed to demonic possession. The people's amazement may have been at seeing that some of the heavenly glory still lingered on the face of Jesus, as it had done upon the face of Moses when he descended from Sinai. *Pineth* away means here becomes rigid, as in an epileptic fit.

The reply of Jesus to the apostles, about prayer and fasting, may reflect that when this account was written the Christian Church was discovering that some types of demons were more difficult to exorcize than others, and that special prayer and fasting were necessary.

LUKE. Luke's account is rather more concise than Mark's. There is no mention of the father's lack of faith, or of the inquiry by the Twelve as to their failure.

MATTHEW. Matthew's version is shorter even than Luke's. The failure of the Twelve is attributed to their lack of faith, rather than to the need for prayer and fasting as in Mark. In v. 20 Jesus tells them that a little faith would achieve much. *A grain of mustard seed* was an expression denoting something small; *uprooting mountains* was a metaphor used by rabbis when speaking about difficulties that seemed insuperable.

97 · The Second Prediction of the Passion

Mark 9$^{30-32}$.
Luke 9$^{43-45}$.
Matthew 17$^{22-23}$

The journey towards Jerusalem has begun. A second time Jesus warns the Twelve about his coming death, but the idea of a suffering Messiah is something that they cannot understand. *After three days* was a Jewish way of saying 'in a short time', just as 'forty' was symbolic of a long time. Notice that Jesus uses the title *Son of man*.

LUKE. In Luke there is no actual mention of Jesus being killed, or of his rising again. Luke probably got his information from some source other than Mark. He suggests that the Twelve failed to understand because God concealed the truth from them.

MATTHEW. Matthew says that the warning was given *while they abode in Galilee*. This is better translated, *while they were gathering themselves together*. It is likely that the Twelve and Jesus split into small groups to avoid attention as they passed through Galilee, and then reassembled.

98 · The Temple Tax

Matthew 17$^{24-27}$

Every male Jew over nineteen years of age was expected to pay a yearly tax of one half-shekel towards the upkeep of the Temple and its costly round of services. The demand was based upon words in Exodus 23^{15}, 30^{13}.

The Greek word translated as *half-shekel* is 'didrachma', that is a double drachma, a Greek silver coin equivalent in value to half a shekel, and about the size of an English florin. There were not many double-drachmas coined, so two Jews might combine to pay the tax in one stater, equivalent to two double-drachmas or one shekel.

Jesus remarked to Peter that perhaps it was inappropriate for them to pay the tax : kings never taxed their own families. Disciples of Jesus were sons of the kingdom of God, and God did not require taxes from them. However, in this case it would only cause misunderstanding to refuse.

Presumably Jesus was in the habit of making the annual payment.

The miracle of the coin in the fish's mouth is unlike the other miracles. In the wilderness Jesus had resisted the temptation to perform miracles to satisfy his own needs or wishes. It is likely here that a suggestion that a little fishing would provide some money has, in the re-telling of the story, become a miracle.

This incident reflects a problem that confronted many Jewish Christians, such as those for whom Matthew was writing. As Christians did they still have to pay the Temple Tax? It was evidently decided still to do so, rather than give offence. After the Temple was destroyed in A.D. 70 the Romans continued the tax for the upkeep of their temple to Jupiter, built in the reconstructed city. Jewish Christians probably thought it wise to pay this also.

99 · Teaching about Humility

Mark 9$^{33-50}$. Luke 9$^{46-50}$, 17$^{1-3}$. Matthew 18$^{1-14}$

The house was possibly Simon Peter's. Jesus taught that the way to real greatness was the way of service to others. The portion of Mark should be compared with Mark 10$^{13-16}$ and with the parable of The Sheep and the Goats.

Many Jews practised exorcism. By the time that this Gospel was written Christians were much aware that non-Christians used the name of Jesus for the purpose. That they should do so was not surprising, because the Christians performed miracles, proclaimed salvation, and baptized converts, *in the name of Jesus* (Acts 2^{38}, 6^{16}, 4^{12}). There is record of magicians also using this new powerful name for their spells (Acts 19$^{13-15}$).

In v. 42 Mark is thinking not only of children in years in the Christian community but of adults who were children or beginners in the Christian Faith. St. Paul used the expression *babes in Christ* in I Corinthians 3^1.

The great millstone was the largest sort in use, and needed an animal to turn it. Sometimes people were put to death in this way.

The injunctions in vv. 43–48 were not meant to be taken literally. Whatever there is that hinders a person from the full service of God needs to be cast out. The hindrance varies with individuals, and the remedy may have to be drastic.

The word translated *hell* is Gehenna. This was the Jewish name for the Valley of Hinnom to the south of Jerusalem. It had once been sacred to the worship of the god Moloch, and children had been burned there as sacrifices. Now it was used as a rubbish-tip and was continually burning. Thus Jews came to use the term Gehenna as a symbol for a place of eternal punishment. (The word hell in the Creeds is not the same. That refers to Hades, a term borrowed by Christians from Greek thought to denote the place of departed spirits.)

In v. 49 *salted* means 'purified'. In v. 50 the disciples of Jesus are bidden to be *salt* in the world. Salt without flavour was useless, so also was a disciple without the true Christian quality to spread in the world (cf. Matthew 5[13]).

LUKE. In Luke the child is not only a suitable object of service but also a pattern of humility. The teaching about offences comes later (Luke 17[1–3]).

MATTHEW. In Matthew the disciples themselves put the question. There is more detail in the teaching about children, e.g. v. 3. The good qualities of children are their love, trust, obedience, sincerity, and humility. These same qualities should mark both a Christian's attitude toward God, the Heavenly Father, and his attitude towards his fellow-men.

As in Mark the words *child* and *little ones* mean those young in years and young in the Faith. Both are to be *received* into the Christian fellowship. Also they are not to be despised (v. 10). In the early Christian community the warning was necessary. At Corinth those who had been given by God particularly spectacular spiritual gifts despised those who appeared to be less blessed (I Corinthians 13[1]). Paul specifically asked them not to despise young Timothy (I Corinthians 16[11]).

Matthew mentions also the angel guardians of such little ones. In Jewish belief angels were specially concerned with the administration of divine justice. In the court of an Eastern king only the most honoured had the privilege of constant access to the king's presence. The angels of God's little ones were similarly favoured.

The parable of The Lost Sheep in vv. 12–14 illustrates God's concern for the lost as well as for the weak. In the early Christian community this could refer to those who strayed away either from the Church or from the Christian way of life.

100 · The Samaritan Villagers   Luke 9⁵¹⁻⁵⁶

Jews travelling from Galilee to Judaea, or vice versa, could travel either to the east of the river Jordan through the district of Peraea, or to the west of Jordan through the hostile district of Samaria. Jesus decided to venture through Samaria. The Samaritans proved hostile, *because his face was as though he were going to Jerusalem.*

The hostility between Jews and Samaritans had a long history. When King Solomon died, the Northern tribes of Israel refused allegiance to his son Rehoboam (I Kings 12²⁰). They chose a king of their own, and became a separate kingdom. Jerusalem and the Temple belonged to the South, so the Northern king made for his people two alternative centres of worship in his own kingdom. He appointed a new priesthood and a revised calendar of feasts. The Jews of the South never forgave him for this.

When the Assyrians invaded Palestine, they defeated the Northern kingdom, carried away captive numbers of the population, and in their place brought in foreigners. The kingdom was then named after its capital city Samaria. Thus the Samaritans became people partly of Jewish and partly of foreign origin.

When the Jews of the South returned from exile in Babylon, and started to rebuild their ruined Temple, the Samaritans offered help, but this was refused because the Jews had adopted a strict anti-foreign attitude. The Samaritans resented this. The Southern Jews too were angry when next the Samaritans built a temple of their own on Mount Gerizim, and later made use of the Greek version of the Jewish Scriptures.

In v. 54 the apostles are thinking of II Kings 1. The words of the rebuke appear in some manuscripts as, *Ye know not what manner of spirit ye are of. For the Son of man came not to destroy men's lives, but to save them.* The name Boanerges probably arose from this incident (Mark 3¹⁷).

V. 51 is an example of the note of triumph that pervades this Gospel. *Received up* links the crucifixion with the ascension.

101 · Would-be Disciples   Luke 9⁵⁷⁻⁶². Matthew 8¹⁸⁻²²

The man who asked leave to go and bury his father was asking permission to carry out one of the most sacred of Jewish obligations. To say farewell to parents was also a duty. Elijah allowed his successor Elisha to do this (I Kings 19²⁰). Perhaps Jesus was thinking of him in v. 62.

Various explanations have been offered to soften the answer: the father was not yet dead, and the son not free from filial responsibility; the reference is to the spiritually dead; the words are a mistranslation of an Aramaic phrase, *Leave the dead to the burier of the dead.* Whatever the precise explanation may be, Jesus clearly expected the work of bringing in the kingdom to rank even before family ties and obligations.

It is unlikely that Jesus expected anyone to follow him there and then literally, since only the apostles were his usual travelling companions and one of the men was given the command, *Go . . . and preach* (Luke 9⁶⁰).

MATTHEW. Matthew's account is briefer. Many scholars think that it is out of chronological order. Jesus' remark about having nowhere to lay his head is much more appropriate during the last journey to Jerusalem, where Luke has put it, than earlier in the ministry at Capernaum where Matthew puts it, for then Jesus had a fixed dwelling-place.

102 · Forgiveness, Faith and Service   Luke 17¹⁻¹⁰

This passage is a collection of sayings. First there is a warning that although *occasions of stumbling* are inevitable, there is *woe unto him* who s the actual cause of others doing wrong, especially when such are the *little ones*, that is the weaker members of the kingdom of God (cf. vv. 1–2 with Mark 9⁴²⁻⁴⁹ and Matthew 18⁶⁻¹⁴, and see Section 99).

Vv. 3–4 deal with the necessity for willing forgiveness (cf. Matthew 18¹⁵⁻³⁵, and see Section 104).

Vv. 5–6 deal with the need for faith. A mustard seed was proverbial for something small. Matthew and Mark speak of faith which will *move mountains* (cf. Matthew 17²⁰ and Mark 11²³ – another proverbial saying). Luke exchanges the mountain for a sycamine (or mulberry) tree, and later Matthew also connects faith with a fig tree (Matthew 21²¹). Possibly Jesus himself used different symbols for faith on different occasions, according to what was easily visible to his hearers.

Vv. 7–10 give the parable of The Unprofitable Servant (see Section 162 No. 8).

103 · The Ten Lepers   Luke 17¹¹⁻¹⁹

Through the midst of (or rather 'in between') means near to the boundary of, Galilee and Samaria. The lepers stand *afar off* because of their disease.

The command in v. 14 was in deference to the Law (Leviticus 14¹⁻³²).

All ten men had faith in Jesus, but only one returned to express gratitude. He was a *stranger*, an alien Samaritan.

104 · Church Discipline   Matthew 18¹⁵⁻³⁵. Luke 17³⁻⁴

Vv. 15–20 of Matthew contain an assortment of Jesus' teaching collected together. The record is coloured by the practice of the Christian community in dealing with offenders at the time when the Gospel was written. The word *brother* means a fellow-Christian.

The passage concerns quarrels between Christians, as opposed to disputes between Christians and non-Christians, in which latter case a Christian was supposed to offer no resistance. If two Christians had quarrelled a few witnesses could be called to help sort the matter out. If this failed, the matter could be brought before the whole congregation. If an offender then refused to listen to the admonition of the 'Church', excommunication was the penalty.

V. 18 confers upon all the Twelve the same authority as was given to Peter at Caesarea Philippi (Matthew 16¹⁹). This meant authority either to restore an offender to Christian fellowship or to excommunicate him.

It is difficult to be sure here of what Jesus originally said, and scholars are not agreed. For example, did he use the word 'Church' (used on only one other occasion: Jesus' reply to Peter, 16¹⁸) to mean a Christian congregation or only the Jewish congregation in a synagogue? Was he looking into the future when his Church would be in being, or merely giving advice to Jewish hearers to make up their quarrels quickly before things went too far (as in the Sermon on the Mount – 5²³⁻²⁶). The mention of two or three witnesses suggests that Jesus had Jewish procedure in mind, for so it was required (Deuteronomy 19¹⁵).

Another problem is, would Jesus refer disparagingly to Gentiles and publicans? Perhaps he was referring to the attitude of a strict Jew simply by way of illustrating the attitude permitted after every effort at reconciliation had been made. One might extend the sentence thus: 'let him be unto thee as the Gentile and the publican would be unto thee.' There is no need to suppose that Jesus was showing his personal feelings.

In vv. 19 and 20 Jesus was adapting a saying of Jewish rabbis, 'when two are sitting and the words of the Torah (Law) are between them, the Shekinah (divine presence) is among them.' The meaning was that the Torah spoke with the immediate authority of God. In his adaptation of the saying, Jesus meant that his presence among his followers would carry an authority similarly divine.

The New Testament writings bear witness to the consciousness of Christians of a divine presence in their midst (Acts 1²⁴, 15²⁸). In Revelations 1¹²⁻²⁰ the risen Son of man is more than present with his Churches: he is their ultimate source of authority.

Until seven times in v. 21 was the teaching of the rabbis. Jesus' *seventy times seven* meant forgiveness unlimited. By way of illustration Matthew includes at this point the parable of The Unmerciful Servant (see Section 160 No. 12).

LUKE. Luke briefly mentions only *seven times in a day*, but this, repeated, would soon lead to the unlimited forgiveness enjoined in Matthew.

105 · Teaching about Marriage and Divorce

Mark 10¹⁻¹². Luke 16¹⁸. Matthew 5²⁷⁻²⁸, ³¹⁻³², 19 ¹⁻¹²

Although only the Fourth Gospel mentions that Jesus went regularly to Jerusalem to attend the Temple festivals, the word *again* makes it clear that this visit is not regarded here as his first.

Jewish Law allowed a man to divorce his wife, *if she find no favour in his eyes, because he hath found some unseemly thing in her* (Deuteronomy 24¹⁻⁴), but the Law did not say what could be considered *some unseemly thing*. There were two main schools of thought as to this in the time of Jesus: the Rabbi Shammai and his following taught that the unseemly thing was adultery, and nothing less; the Rabbi Hillel taught that many lesser faults could be counted.

Jesus, asked which of the two views he favoured, rejected both. In vv. 6–8 he reminded his questioners that, since God created male and female, he regarded two married people not as two distinct individuals but as one complementary and indissoluble whole.

In Jewish Law usually the husband only could divorce the wife. Roman Law permitted a wife also to divorce her husband, but this was likely to happen only in cases where the woman was not dependent upon her husband financially. It may well be that in v. 12 Jesus was thinking of Herodias, whose divorce was a public scandal at the time (see Section 84). By Roman standards Jewish practice might seem to be unfair to a wife, but since Jewish Law required that there must be *some unseemly thing* before divorce, this was an improvement upon more primitive practice wherein a man could simply tell his wife to go.

The comment of Jesus about *hardness of heart* meant that in the days of Moses God permitted divorce because people could not then understand any better.

Jewish Law not only allowed divorce but also permitted re-marriage after divorce. This was a necessity for a poor woman with no means of livelihood. In vv. 11 and 12 Jesus said that re-marriage after divorce was

91

the sin of adultery. His teaching was thus far more strict than that of Shammai, Hillel, or even the Law of Moses.

It is sometimes suggested that Jesus did not teach this strict 'no divorce or re-marriage rule', but that it originated in the early Christian Church. But from where would the Church get so strict a view, if not from him? The first Christians were people who, whether Jew or Gentile, had previously accepted divorce and re-marriage? Would they suddenly become more strict upon their own initiative?

The standard of life demanded by Jesus was never easy, whether he was speaking of marriage, or saying such things as *judge not*, or *love your enemies*, or *love your neighbour as yourself.*

LUKE. Luke's single verse on the subject is almost the same as Mark 10^{11-12}.

MATTHEW. In Matthew's account of the question concerning divorce, the words *for every cause* are added to the question, and an important detail is added to the answer (19^9). This on the face of it looks as though Jesus did agree with the teaching of Shammai. The most straightforward explanation is that someone, copying the Gospel of Matthew by hand, added the phrase *except for fornication* deliberately, to soften the impact, or accidentally. Mark and Luke do not mention it.

The Revised Version marginal note gives an alternative reading: *saving for the cause of fornication, maketh her an adulteress.* Some ancient authorities support this reading. Also it is how the teaching of Jesus is reported in the Sermon on the Mount (5^{32}).

Does this make a difference? In English 'fornication' means unchastity before marriage, and 'adultery' means unchastity after. Jesus therefore would appear to be teaching that a man who divorced his wife would make her an adulteress (since most probably she would have to marry again in order to exist) but that, if he divorced her because she had been unchaste before marriage, his only offence would be in divorcing her. Jesus would thus be pointing out the weakness of the Jewish Law: a man who, under Jewish Law, divorced his wife, actually compelled her, and her new partner, to commit adultery.

The reading in 19^9 as it stands can also be interpreted thus: A man who divorces his wife and marries again commits adultery, but, if a man *puts away* his wife because of her fornication before marriage, he himself does not commit adultery if he marries again, because his first marriage was no real marriage. It thus becomes a case not of divorce but of nullity. According to Jewish Law fornication made a subsequent marriage null and void.

Thus the Christian ruling in this matter is that re-marriage after divorce is wrong (see I Corinthians 7^{10-17}, the earliest record of Jesus' teaching), but that re-marriage after a decree of nullity is permitted, since such is not actually re-marriage. (The more advanced student who wishes to pursue this problem further should study the possible meanings of the Greek words 'porneia' and 'moicheia', translated as 'fornication' and 'adultery' in our English Bible.)

Vv. 10–12 contain teaching to be found only in Matthew. V. 11 raises the problem, does it refer back to the teaching about divorce and re-marriage. If it does, there could be two alternative interpretations: Jesus admitted that, although his teaching was the ideal, it set too hard a moral standard for many; the words may have been added by the writer (or copyist) as a comment, and not have been spoken by Jesus.

It is possible, however, that *this saying* refers to v. 12, and that there we have a separate item of teaching, grouped by the writer, as was typical of him, with the divorce and re-marriage question. There is much to be said for this. In the early Church the question often arose as to whether it was better to marry or remain single. The first Christians expected Jesus to return in their own lifetime, and this influenced their attitude towards the question. Jesus may well have been asked whether the unmarried state were not the ideal, and given the reply, *All men cannot receive this saying.* In v. 29 Jesus does point out the need for giving up everything for his sake.

Numerous New Testament writings deal with this matter, and the advice in them is probably based on the teaching of Jesus (cf. Luke 20³⁵, I Corinthians 7¹⁻⁷, Revelation 14⁴).

106 · Jesus Blesses the Children   Mark 10¹³⁻¹⁶. Luke 18¹⁵⁻¹⁷. Matthew 19¹³⁻¹⁵

In Mark's account (and in Matthew) this incident comes immediately after the teaching about divorce and re-marriage, and not perhaps by mere coincidence. The women who brought their children to Jesus may have heard the teaching, and felt that here was a rabbi who recognized a woman's need for security and a permanent home.

When the disciples did not wish Jesus to be bothered by a lot of small children, he spoke again about the need for humility on the part of those who wished to enter the kingdom of God (see Section 99). The kingdom of God, moreover, was not something to be earned, as it were, by personal merit: it was God's gift, to be *received* with all the gratitude, trust, and humility of a child.

LUKE. The only difference between Luke's account and Mark's, is that

93

Luke omits mention of the rebuke of the disciples. The omission is possibly due to the fact that by the time that Luke and Matthew wrote their Gospels, the Twelve were revered personages, and some of them martyrs. So their shortcomings, bluntly told by Mark, get softened.

In Luke the incident does not follow the teaching about marriage.

MATTHEW. Matthew as well as Luke omits mention of Jesus' indignation. He also omits the teaching about *receiving* the kingdom.

107 · The Rich Young Ruler   Mark 10$^{17-31}$. Luke 18$^{18-30}$. Matthew 19$^{16-30}$

Jesus loved the man's eagerness, and obvious sincerity, but wished him to give more thought to the words that he used. The Twelve were surprised that anything could be hard for the rich, both because they themselves were poor, and many Jews regarded riches as a special blessing bestowed by God. Jesus did not say that wealth is wrong, but that wealth makes entry into the kingdom difficult, because the owner is open to temptations to greed, selfishness, and indulgence (cf. Luke 16$^{19-31}$).

The saying about a camel (sometimes an elephant) was an Eastern expression used to indicate something impossible. It is exaggerated, and not meant to be taken literally. Two other explanations are sometimes given:

(1) That there was a small gate into Jerusalem called 'the needle's eye', through which a laden camel could not go. (There is no real evidence for this.) The explanation may have developed from Jesus' teaching that people laden with riches found entry into the kingdom difficult.

(2) The word *camel* is intended to be a camel's halter or rope, and the saying used by Jesus referred to threading a needle with rope.

V. 27 sums up the whole truth of redemption: men cannot be saved by their own efforts; salvation is the generous gift of God. *Now in this time* in v. 30 refers presumably to the new associations gained in the family of Christ and his Church.

LUKE. Luke tells us that the rich man was a ruler (probably of the local synagogue). His account follows Mark, except that he does not mention that Jesus loved the man, and that the disciples were *amazed*.

MATTHEW. Matthew has re-written Mark's account, and in particular has rephrased the question and answer. Presumably Matthew felt that the reply might be taken to mean that Jesus knew that he was not good (this has been suggested by a few scholars), instead of its being a deliberate effort by Jesus to make the man think of his words. The sinlessness of Jesus is a truth never questioned in the New Testament.

Matthew adds to the list of the commandments, *Thou shalt love thy neighbour as thyself*. He also gives the information that the man was young. (In Mark this is implied in the statement there that he *ran*.)

In v. 28 Matthew, writing for Jewish Christians, is pointing out that, as the twelve sons of Israel formed the Old Israel, so the twelve apostles were the beginning of the New Israel, the Christian Church. The idea that the righteous would judge the world was no new one in Jewish thought. That the Son of man would sit *on the throne of his glory* refers to the Jewish and early Christian belief that after the Messianic judgement God would create a new heaven and a new earth (Isaiah 65^{17}, Revelation 20^{11}–21^{1}).

The parable of The Labourers in the Vineyard (20$^{1-16}$) seems intended to illustrate the warning in 19^{30}, but the illustration is not completely apt, because all the labourers, both first and last, receive the same reward. (For the meaning of the parable, recorded only by Matthew, see Section 160 No. 10).

108 · The Third Prediction of the Passion

Mark 10$^{32-34}$.
Luke 18$^{31-34}$.
Matthew 20$^{17-19}$

The Twelve were *amazed* as Jesus strode grimly ahead, and *afraid* because they sensed impending danger. The detail in vv. 33–34 may be due to the fact that, by the time that Mark wrote, the events had taken place. On the other hand it would be easy to anticipate the likely course of things.

Each time that Jesus spoke of his coming death the disciples were slow to understand. The idea that the Messiah would suffer was far from their minds. After the first prediction Peter rebuked Jesus; after the second prediction the Twelve argued about who should be greatest in the kingdom; after the third James and John attempted to reserve the best places (see next section).

LUKE. Luke's account follows that of Mark, except for the addition of *all things that are written by the prophets shall be accomplished*. Jesus realized that the Scriptures indicated his coming death as part of his role as the Suffering-Servant Messiah. The Twelve never realized this

95

until after the resurrection, when Jesus himself pointed it out to them (Luke 24$^{25-27,\ 46-47}$).

Luke makes no mention of how the Twelve were *amazed* and *afraid*, probably because he tends to emphasize more the glory than the tragedy of Jesus' life.

MATTHEW. Matthew's account is an abridged version of Mark. Like Luke he omits mention of how the Twelve were *amazed* and *afraid*.

109 · The Request of James and John
Mark 10$^{35-45}$.
Matthew 20$^{20-28}$

The request, coming immediately after the third prediction of the Passion, shows how the Twelve, despite all warnings, were still hoping for earthly glory. *Cup* is symbolic of suffering, as in Isaiah 51$^{17,\ 22}$ and Mark 14^{36}; *baptism* is symbolic of death (Romans 6$^{3-4}$).

James was the first of the Twelve to suffer martyrdom: he was put to death by Herod Agrippa I (Acts 12^1). One tradition (supported by this story) says that John also died at the same time, but another says that, after persecution and exile, he lived to a great age at Ephesus, and died peacefully.

There is a difference of opinion over v. 45. Either it is a Christian comment on the previous verses, in order to emphasize Jesus' supreme example of service; or the words were spoken by Jesus himself in the role of the Suffering-Servant Messiah (cf. the Fourth Servant Song, and especially Isaiah 53$^{11-12}$).

It is impossible to know how sure Jesus was beforehand that his death would indeed take place. Nevertheless it would seem to be clear that Jesus did realize that he would have to die for his cause (for the authorities would not let him continue unchallenged), that he thought of his death as part of God's plan as seen in the Scriptures, and that he believed that his death would in some way benefit others, as a *ransom* or deliverance.

MATTHEW. Matthew's account follows that of Mark, but it is noticeable that the mother of James and John makes the request. Jesus' reply, however, is not addressed to her, but to them. Thus Matthew apparently tries to spare the two brothers by putting the blame for their ambitious request upon their mother. Her name was probably Salome, and it is possible that she was the sister of Mary, the mother of Jesus. If this was so, James and John may have felt that family ties gave them the right to make their request.

110 · Blind Bartimaeus

Mark 10⁴⁶⁻⁵². Luke 18³⁵⁻⁴³.
Matthew 20²⁹⁻³⁴

Jericho, the city of palm trees, was the last city on the route to Jerusalem. A blind beggar, the son of Timaeus, (i.e. Bar Timaeus) learning that Jesus was passing, cried aloud, *Jesus, thou son of David.* This was the first time (according to the Synoptic Gospels) that any Jew, apart from the Twelve, had called Jesus the Messiah. The Messiah was expected to be a descendant of King David. So *Son of David* was a title meaning Messiah.

The people standing near resented the interruption, and perhaps thought the language rather rash in an enemy-occupied country, and within fifteen miles of the capital, but Jesus, in healing the man, said nothing about keeping quiet about his being the Messiah. The time for secrecy was over.

LUKE. Luke says that Jesus healed Bartimaeus on the way into Jericho, whereas Mark says that the incident took place as Jesus was leaving. Luke does not mention the beggar's name.

MATTHEW. In Matthew's account there are two blind beggars. It is not unusual in this Gospel to find two people in a miracle story, instead of the one mentioned by Mark (e.g. Matthew 8²⁸⁻³⁴). This is partly because Matthew tries to emphasize the miracles, and partly because he sometimes combines two similar stories. In this instance Matthew may have heard one story which said that a blind man was healed as Jesus entered Jericho (the one that Luke wrote down), and another story which said that a blind man was healed as Jesus left (the one that Mark recorded). Thus two stories about one man probably became one story about two men.

111 · Zacchaeus the Tax-Collector

Luke 19¹⁻¹⁰

The sycomore tree was not the same as an English sycamore: it bore fruit like figs, and leaves like mulberry leaves. Probably the swaying of this fig-mulberry tree attracted Jesus' attention, and the humour of the situation appealed to him.

Jesus' concern for yet another publican and 'sinner' caused many to murmur. His interest in such people must often have lost for him many followers among those who professed better principles. Zacchaeus' promise to repay fourfold was based on Exodus 22¹ (with Jesus' comment cf. Mark 2¹³⁻¹⁷).

Holy Week

112 · The Triumphal Entry into Jerusalem

Mark 11$^{1-11}$.
Luke 19$^{29-40}$.
Matthew 21 $^{1-11}$

According to the Synoptic Gospels Jesus made no public proclamation of his being the Messiah until this point in his ministry. Now the time had come for him to make his claim openly, and in the capital, the headquarters of the Jewish authorities. If, however, his claim resulted in his death, which was more than likely, he wanted it to be clear that he died because of his claim, and not merely as a trouble-maker.

It seems likely, therefore, that Jesus chose to make his claim in action, rather than in words, by deliberately fulfilling a prophecy in Zechariah 9^9 (not quoted in Mark). This is one of the few mentions in the Old Testament of a peaceful king, and Jesus wanted to make it plain that he was a peaceful Messiah. A king going into battle would ride a horse, but an ass or mule was usual in peacetime.

It seems evident from the Gospel that Jesus had already made arrangements with someone to provide an ass. The words *the Lord hath need of him* sound like a password. (This is further indication that Jesus was already known in the region of Jerusalem.)

That Jesus began his ride from the Mount of Olives has possibly some significance. It provides another link with Zechariah (14^4) in which the unknown prophet declares that, when all seems lost, God himself will come and establish his kingdom. At such time, however, according to the prophet, God would come to fight. Jesus came in peace.

That the ass had not been ridden before possibly emphasized a special occasion for a special rider.

How far the ordinary people understood the meaning of Jesus' action is not clear, and scholars dispute the point. Possibly some people realized the implications of his 'Triumphal Entry'; others were content simply to welcome the prophet from Galilee, after the manner of II Kings 9^{13}, I Maccabees 13^{51}, II Maccabees 10$^{1-8}$. Only the Fourth Gospel says that the branches were cut from palm trees.

One psalm closely associated with the Feast of Tabernacles was Psalm 118. In it (v. 25) are the words, *Save now, we beseech thee . . . Blessed is he that cometh in the name of the Lord.* The cry *Hosanna* comes from this psalm, and means *Save now*. When the psalm was used at the Feast of Tabernacles, branches were waved at the word *Hosanna*. Consequently the branches themselves were called Hosannas. The words *Hosanna in the highest* would mean 'Help from heaven'.

As well as being used at the Feast of Tabernacles, this psalm was sung as a welcome to pilgrims. It was natural therefore that the crowd should welcome Jesus with these words. Nevertheless the words *Blessed is he that cometh . . .*, though used as a welcome to pilgrims generally, on this occasion seemed to be directed at Jesus in particular. It is possible that the words had already become associated with the coming of the Messiah.

According to Mark the incident ended suddenly and vaguely.

LUKE. Luke's account closely follows that of Mark, but notice the difference in the cry of the crowd, *Blessed is the King that cometh . . . peace in heaven* (instead of *Hosanna*), *and glory in the highest* (instead of *Hosanna in the highest*). There is no mention of the branches.

But Luke mentions a protest by the Pharisees, and a refusal by Jesus to quieten his disciples.

MATTHEW. Matthew quotes the prophecy in Zechariah 9⁹, and this mentions *an ass, and upon a colt the foal of an ass.* To relate the incident to the prophecy more exactly, Matthew puts two animals into his story. Actually the prophecy refers to only one animal, for *a colt the foal of an ass* is but poetic repetition of *an ass*, that is, the same animal.

Matthew adds to the shout of the crowd the words, *Son of David* (i.e. Messiah). In this he reflects the way in which the incident came to be regarded in the Christian community. The crowd, when asked at the time by the residents of Jerusalem, *Who is this?* replied simply, *This is the prophet, Jesus, from Nazareth of Galilee.*

Summary

Students will find that scholars hold varying and sometimes contradictory views as to the implications of this story:

(1) Jesus was definitely claiming to be the Messiah. Some scholars say that Jesus was not claiming to be the Messiah, for Mark does not mention the Zechariah prophecy, which is said to have inspired Jesus' action. (Nevertheless Mark has the *Mount of Olives* link with Zechariah.)

(2) Jesus had made previous arrangements to borrow the ass. Some scholars say that Jesus had not made such arrangements: the whole affair was spontaneous.

(3) The crowd welcomed Jesus as the Messiah, and their cry *Hosanna*

was an appeal to Jesus to save them from the Romans. Some scholars say that the crowd welcomed Jesus only as a great prophet. The words of the psalm were used merely as a psalm of welcome. Only Matthew records the words, *Son of David.* The incident gained Messianic significance because of Christian interpretation.

The more general view, however, is the one set out above in the Mark section.

113 · The Lament over Jerusalem Luke 19⁴¹⁻⁴⁴

In striking contrast to the excitement of the disciples and the pilgrims was the lament of Jesus over the city of Jerusalem; it was a very patriotic Jesus who grieved for his people and thought of their future. He seems to have had in mind the song of the Jewish exiles as they too had once wept by the waters of Babylon (Psalm 137).

The words of Jesus were fulfilled in A.D. 70 when the armies of Titus destroyed the city, and the Temple was burned (cf. Luke 13³⁴, ³⁵ and Matthew 23 ³⁷⁻³⁹).

114 · The Cleansing of the Temple Mark 11¹⁵⁻¹⁹. Luke 19⁴⁵⁻⁴⁸. Matthew 21¹²⁻¹⁷

Jesus had entered the city as a Messiah of peace, but as a Messiah of judgement he would purge the Temple of abuses. It is likely that he was inspired by Malachi 3¹⁻³.

In the Court of the Gentiles was a market for the sale to pilgrims of sacrificial animals. In the Law of Moses were strict rules regarding what they should be (Exodus 12⁵). The animals sold in the market were guaranteed to fulfil all the requirements. Consequently high prices were charged.

There were also money-changers who changed heathen Gentile money, brought by Jewish pilgrims from all parts of the Roman Empire, into the coinage approved at the Temple. No other coins could be offered, because many foreign coins bore upon them the likenesses of heathen gods. The money-changers, because of the great demand, were able to charge a high rate of exchange.

The profits from the market went, not to the people directly in charge of it, but to the chief priests.

Many of the great Jewish writers had seen Israel as destined to be the means whereby God would become known to the whole world:

Gentiles of all nations would seek the God of Israel (Isaiah 2³, Zechariah 8²³). But ever since the return from Exile in Babylon the official Jewish attitude towards foreigners had become increasingly indifferent. So the bad impression that this trading must have given to Gentile visitors, and possible converts, was ignored.

In great indignation Jesus strode into the Court of the Gentiles. Above the commotion he shouted *Is it not written, My house shall be called a house of prayer for all the nations?* He quoted from Isaiah 56⁷ (i.e. Third Isaiah), and Jeremiah 7¹¹, who also had made protest about the Temple. In view of the site of the market the words *for all the nations* were very apt. The incident happened so quickly that the Temple police could not intervene.

Some scholars say that Jesus' action did not necessarily indicate a claim to Messiahship: he did what any loyal Jew should have done, and he was but quoting the prophets when he said, *My house . . .* On the other hand, he could have been using the words personally, and, taken along with the Triumphal Entry, his action does become significant.

It should be noted that in the Fourth Gospel the Cleansing of the Temple is put at the beginning of the ministry. This is one of the important differences between the Fourth Gospel and the Synoptic.

LUKE. Luke does not say when the cleansing of the Temple took place, whether on the same day as the Triumphal Entry, or on the next day as in Mark. His account is much briefer than Mark's.

MATTHEW. In Matthew's account the cleansing of the Temple is made the climax of the Triumphal Entry. He also mentions that sick people came to Jesus in the Temple to be healed, and that children continued to cry *Hosanna*. The scribes and chief priests protested to Jesus, but he made no attempt to stop the children, and quoted Psalm 8² to justify them. (Cf. Luke 19³⁹ where it is the disciples whom Jesus is asked to silence.)

115 · The Fruitless Fig Tree

Mark 11¹²⁻¹⁴, ²⁰⁻²⁴.
Matthew 21¹⁸⁻²²

This story presents some difficulty. That Jesus should curse a tree for being fruitless, at a time of year when it could not be otherwise, seems inconsistent with his character as shown in the Gospels. There are various explanations and interpretations:

(1) Luke does not mention this particular incident, but he mentions a parable told by Jesus in which a fig tree represented Israel, unfruitful and deserving to be destroyed (Luke 13⁶⁻⁹). When therefore Jesus saw

this particular fig tree, with a profusion of leaves falsely suggesting an early fruiting, he remarked upon it as an illustration of his previous parable.

(2) Jesus saw a withered fig tree, and used that to illustrate his parable.

(3) Jesus and the Twelve passed both a green tree and a withered tree. He compared them. In the constant re-telling of the incident by Christians, the two trees became one, and the occasion a miracle.

(4) Since the story in Mark leads on to a discourse on prayer (vv. 22–25) the blasting of the fig tree may have been an actual miracle, to demonstrate the power of faith. Against this is the fact that Jesus did not usually work miracles to emphasize his teaching (but cf. Mark 2³⁻¹²).

(5) Jesus cursed the tree as a symbolic action, demonstrating the wrath of God against ostentation and non-fulfilment. (Old Testament prophets sometimes made use of symbolic actions: e.g. I Kings 22¹¹, Jeremiah 19¹⁰⁻¹¹). It is to be noted that Jesus displayed no personal anger.

(6) The blasting of the fig tree was a piece of dramatic irony, in which the tree represented Jesus, himself on the way to being destroyed. There is a likely reference to Jesus as a *green tree* in Luke 23³¹.

MATTHEW. In Matthew the fig tree incident is not divided by the account of the cleansing of the Temple: the tree withers away immediately while the Twelve watch it. In this Gospel its purpose is stated definitely to demonstrate the power of faith.

116 · By What Authority?   Mark 11²⁷⁻³³. Luke 20¹⁻⁸. Matthew 21²³⁻²⁷

The enemies of Jesus were seeking from Jesus a definite admission that he claimed to be the Messiah, or some statement that would offend the Romans. The different sects who brought the questions usually had little to do with one another. Now they banded together in a common desire to get rid of Jesus.

The question as to authority was put by representatives of the Jewish supreme council, the Sanhedrin. They had, of course, every right to ask Jesus by what authority he had cleansed the Court of the Gentiles, but they did not really want to know this: already they had decided that he must die.

Jesus' question about John the Baptist was not an evasion, but a skilful way of making the questioners answer their own question. When they made up their minds about John's authority (and this they had, although they did not care to admit it) they would know Jesus' authority, for they were one and the same. Incidentally this was a claim by Jesus to be the Messiah, because John regarded himself as the herald of the Messiah.

LUKE and MATTHEW. Both accounts follow that of Mark.

117 · The Wicked Husbandmen   Mark 12$^{1-12}$. Luke 20$^{9-19}$. Matthew 21 $^{33-46}$

This is not so much a parable as an allegory, because there is significance in many of the details of the story. The watch tower was for guarding the crop against thieves during harvest time. A vineyard had been an accepted symbol for the Jewish nation for centuries, at least since Isaiah had composed his famous parable or Song of the Vineyard (Isaiah 5$^{1-7}$). Indeed Jesus' parable was very likely based upon that of Isaiah. As soon as he began therefore his hearers would think of the vineyard as representing the Jewish nation, and the owner as representing God.

As Jesus told his story, the owner's servants were the prophets, most of whom had suffered persecution in some way; the husbandmen or tenant-farmers were the chief priests, scribes, and elders; the owner's son was the Messiah, whose death was even then being plotted. The destruction of the *husbandmen* was fulfilled when Jerusalem was destroyed in A.D. 70; the giving of the vineyard to others occurred even as Mark wrote, because all that was noblest in the Jewish heritage of faith was taken over by, and had found fulfilment in, the new Israel, the Christian Church.

Psalm 118 is mentioned again, this time by Jesus, who quoted vv. 22–23. The stone rejected represented Israel, despised by other nations, yet capable of restoration as one of the most important in a building. It is very likely that by the time of Jesus these words were applied not only to Israel the nation, but to the nation's representative, the Messiah. The early Christians so used it (Acts 4^{11}, Ephesians 2^{20}, I Peter 2^{7}). The enemies of Jesus could not fail to suspect that his words implied a claim to be the Messiah, and were also an accusation against them.

Some scholars say that, though the son in the story represents the Messiah, Jesus did not necessarily mean that he was the son. Others suggest that the son is intended to be John the Baptist, and that any idea that Jesus thus claimed to be the Messiah is due to the way in which the Christian Church had presented the story. It should be borne in mind here, however, that although Jesus' claims to be the Messiah may have been written down more precisely because they were written down by people sure in that belief, the Church would not invent, on behalf of her founder, claims that he had never made.

A third suggestion is that the parable was invented by the Church for use in controversy with the Jews. The reasons given are (1) Jesus anticipates his death; (2) He claims to be greater than the prophets. Reason (1), however, ignores the other predictions mentioned by Mark, but, even if they were not made, Jesus well knew that his days were numbered. Moreover, if the parable were invented by the Church after Jesus' death, it was invented also after his resurrection, yet there is no hint of that in the parable (although, perhaps, such a hint in the quotation from Psalm 118). Reason (2) is not very strong: if Jesus claimed to be the Messiah, a claim to be greater than the prophets was unavoidable.

LUKE. Luke's account closely follows that of Mark. V. 18 is an addition based on Nebuchadnezzar's dream (Daniel 2^{31-45}), on the stone of stumbling mentioned by Isaiah (Isaiah 8^{14}), and on the stone of sure foundation (Isaiah 28^{16} and see Romans 9^{32-33}, Ephesians 2^{20}, I Peter 2^{6-7}).

MATTHEW. Matthew closely follows Mark. The enemies of Jesus themselves pronounce judgement upon the wicked husbandmen, in reply to Jesus' question in v. 40. In v. 43 Jesus plainly tells the Jews that the kingdom will be taken from them. V. 44 is also an addition to Mark. (For explanation see Luke section.)

118 · Tax Paid to Caesar
Mark 12^{13-17}. Luke 20^{20-26}. Matthew 22^{15-22}

The question was put by the Pharisees, the religious, and the Herodians, the political party among the Jews. It was not the first time that they had combined against Jesus (Mark 3^6).

The coin was a Roman silver denarius (from which we get the symbol 'd' for pence). The likeness, name, or symbol of the ruler by whom a coin was issued was a guarantee of its worth. People who made use of it were at least that much under obligation to him. In a sense the coin could be said to be his. The question was a trap, but the answer was no evasion. Jews had to pay a double tax, one to the Temple and one to Rome. Jesus said therefore, Pay both taxes; give both Caesar and God their dues. Since the Herodians approved of the one, and the Pharisees of the other, neither could take offence.

It was right that Jews should pay towards their Temple, and not unfair that they should pay something to Rome, from which they derived undoubted administrative benefits. Nevertheless many felt the Roman tax to be offensive: it was a continual reminder that the Jews were not a free nation.

Other explanations of Jesus' answer are sometimes given:

(1) Jesus refused to enter into a matter of politics and give an opinion. His questioners admitted that they were making use of coins bearing Caesar's image and name; very well then; Caesar was entitled to something in return. At the same time, giving Caesar his due did not preclude the fulfilment of obligations to God.

(2) Jesus did get involved in politics. The Pharisees had brought direct Roman rule upon the nation by refusing to support Herod Archelaus as their king. They therefore deserved to have to *Render unto Caesar*. The Herodians, supporters of Herod Antipas, were prepared to compromise on religious matters. Herod Antipas was permitted by the Romans to rule on condition that there was no attempt to make Jewish converts, and that he allowed temples for Emperor-worship, and images of the Emperor, throughout the land. So, well might the Herodians be told to render things due to God.

LUKE and MATTHEW. Luke and Matthew closely follow Mark.

119 · A Question about Life after Death

Mark 12¹⁸⁻²⁷.
Luke 20²⁷⁻⁴⁰.
Matthew 22²³⁻³³

Sadducees did not believe in a life after death, or in the existence of angels. Scholars say that this sort of question was probably often debated by Sadducees and Pharisees. It was put to Jesus in an exaggerated form in the hope of making him look foolish in a learned discussion.

The question turned on the Jewish practice of Levirate marriage (Deuteronomy 25⁵⁻¹⁰). If a man died childless, it was the duty of his brother or next-of-kin to marry the wife. The first child born was then the dead man's heir. (The story of Ruth is a good example.) By the time of Jesus the practice was probably obsolete.

The reason for the practice in the first instance was a primitive and uncertain view about life after death. A man's immortality depended upon the family's name being continued, and upon there being someone to remember him.

Jesus pointed out that marriage is something for this world only: in the next world people are spiritual beings as are the angels. Jesus then pointed out to the Sadducees their error in not believing in a future life. They would accept only religious beliefs based upon Scripture; very well then: even the Law of Moses, the most venerated part of the Jewish Scripture, gave evidence of life after death. In the story of the burning bush (Exodus 3²⁻⁶) God said, not 'I was the God', but *I am the God* . . . as though the patriarchs still existed for him. They had lived on earth centuries before Moses.

This was a type of Scripture argument popular at the time. The important thing for us is that Jesus was arguing for a belief in life after death.

LUKE and MATTHEW. These accounts closely follow Mark.

120 · The Most Important Commandment

Mark 12²⁸⁻³⁴.
Luke 10²⁵⁻³⁷.
Matthew 22³⁴⁻⁴⁰

This question was possibly a sincere one. The Jewish Law contained 248 positive commands, and 365 negative commands. Some rabbis had tried to summarize all these commandments, and some had tried to distinguish between moral law and ceremonial law, saying that the moral law was the more important.

Jesus answered the question in the familiar words of the Shema (Deuteronomy 6⁴⁻⁵) and by quoting Leviticus 19¹⁸. The point is not certain, but it is possible that Jesus was the first to link these two commands together. For Jews, however, *neighbour* would mean only other Jews. The scribe's words in v. 33 recall the teaching of great prophets such as Amos, Hosea, and Isaiah, who stressed the importance of doing right as well as offering sacrifices.

LUKE. In Luke the question was put on a different occasion (after the return of the seventy) and in the style of the rich young ruler. Luke uses for *scribe* the word 'lawyer'. In Luke it is the lawyer who quotes the Shema, adding the phrase from Leviticus, and Jesus agrees with him (instead of the reverse as in Mark). The lawyer was *tempting* Jesus, that is testing his opinion.

To show that *neighbour* is not to be restricted to Jews, Luke adds one of his own collection of parables, with a foreigner as its hero. The priest and Levite were probably anxious about their safety. Since they were *going down that way* they were travelling away from the Temple, and could have no excuse that they would possibly be late for service, or that contact with the man, if dead, would make them ceremonially unclean and unfit for duty. Oil and wine were used for dressing wounds. Luke shows his medical interest. The two pence were two denarii. The road from Jerusalem to Jericho is about fifteen miles long. The lawyer avoided using the hated word *Samaritan*.

MATTHEW. In Matthew the scribe is one of the Pharisees; the question comes in the same setting as Mark's, but the account is more brief, and there is no comment upon Jesus' answer.

121 · Christ, the Son of David?   Mark 12³⁵⁻³⁷. Luke 20⁴¹⁻⁴⁴. Matthew 22⁴¹⁻⁴⁶

It is difficult to decide exactly what Jesus meant to teach by this question.

According to Jewish belief, the Messiah would be descended from David (e.g. Isaiah 11¹). The scribes in particular stressed this characteristic of the Messiah, but was it not perhaps the least important of the Messiah's qualifications? This, possibly, was what Jesus hoped to point out. While the scribes thought of the Messiah in such a limited way, they were not likely to recognize in Jesus the fulfilment of the Suffering-Servant Messiah prophecies.

Jesus used Scripture (Psalm 110) in the academic way common among rabbis. David *in the Spirit* means David inspired by the Spirit.

An alternative explanation, though not so likely, is that Jesus was arguing that the Messiah was not descended from David at all. According to Matthew and Luke, Jesus himself was so descended (Matthew 1¹⁻¹⁷, Luke 3²³⁻³⁸).

It is usually thought that Psalm 110 was written long after David, probably in the days of the Maccabees. But this does not affect the point that Jesus tried to make, that Scripture as it was read showed that the title Son of David suggested too limited an idea of the Messiah.

LUKE. Luke closely follows Mark.

MATTHEW. Matthew says that the question was put by Jesus to the Pharisees, and writes it in a different form. The rest of his account follows Mark.

122 · Faults of Scribes and Pharisees   Mark 12³⁸⁻⁴⁰. Luke 20⁴⁵⁻⁴⁷ (11³⁷⁻⁵⁴). Matthew 23¹⁻³⁶

The warning was given in the Temple. It is not certain what is meant by *they which devour widows' houses*. Possibly scribes when consulted as lawyers, especially in matters concerning a widow's property, charged very high fees.

LUKE. Luke's account in Chapter 20 follows Mark's, but he reports in Chapter 11 a more detailed criticism. The occasion was a meal in a Pharisee's house to which Jesus had been invited. Jesus often came into conflict with scribes and Pharisees, but severity may have been added to this denunciation by the early Christians, who found in the Jews bitter opponents.

V. 42 refers to the obligation for Jews to pay to God a tithe, or tenth part, of their harvest and their flocks (Leviticus 27[30-33]). So anxious were Pharisees to observe this law precisely that they carefully took a tenth part of even the tiniest herbs. At the same time more important matters, such as *judgement and the love of God*, were overlooked.

V. 43 condemns their love of outward show. V. 44 compares them to tombs so overgrown that people were unaware of their existence, and became defiled by unintentional contact with the dead.

From v. 45 onwards scribes or lawyers are included in the denunciation. Many of them were Pharisees.

To *bring blood* upon a person or people was to impute guilt and blame. Christians reading this Gospel would think of how the Jews suffered when the Romans destroyed their city and Temple. The *blood of Abel* is mentioned in Genesis 4[10], and the *blood of Zachariah* (or Zechariah) is recorded in II Chronicles 24[22]. Zachariah was the son of Jehoiada the high priest, and he was slain in the Temple precincts. He prophesied that God would forsake his people because they had forsaken him. Thus the mention of Abel and Zachariah spanned all Jewish recorded history.

It is possible that the author of the Gospel had in mind another Zachariah, the son of Baruch. He was a great lover of justice and liberty. A mob lynched him in the Temple because it was thought that he had betrayed Jerusalem to the Romans. Jesus himself could not have referred to this Zachariah, since he was killed in A.D. 70.

MATTHEW. Matthew is much more detailed than Mark and Luke 20[45-47]. His account has much in common with Luke 11[37-54], being if anything more detailed still, although, unlike Luke, the setting is not a Pharisee's house. The denunciation in Matthew is so harsh that the report has possibly been influenced by the bitter conflict that raged between Jews and Christians in the period when the Gospel was written.

The scribes sat *on Moses' seat* because they spoke as his successors (vv. 1-4). In effect Jesus advised: Do as they say but not as they do.

A phylactery (vv. 5-12) is a small leather box, worn by Jews on the forehead and the left arm during morning prayer (cf. Exodus 13[9, 16]). It contains four small pieces of parchment, with a passage from Scripture upon each (Exodus 13$^{1-10, 11-16}$, Deuteronomy 6$^{4-9}$, 11$^{13-21}$ – part of the Shema). The borders or tassels were prescribed by the Law (Numbers 15^{38}, Deuteronomy 22^{12}).

It has been suggested that the command to avoid titles originated in the early Christian Church as a result of the constant repetition of the teaching of Jesus that the greatest were those who served others, and out of regard by Christians for Jesus as their only rabbi or teacher, and for God as their Father (see Section 99).

The Seven Woes

The word *Hypocrite* means a play-actor. In the Greek theatre of the time, players wore masks to conceal their own characters and to portray others. Thus the word comes to mean someone who conceals his true character.

(1) In the early Church the words in v. 13 would apply to Jews in general, who did all that they could to prevent converts from entering the Church.

(2) V. 15 refers to the missionary activity undertaken mainly by Jews of the Dispersion (that is, Jews dispersed throughout the empire). They were rather more broadminded than Palestinian Jews. Their synagogues had each a circle of converts known as Godfearers: they were people learning about the Jewish religion, but as yet bound only by food laws and Sabbath laws. The next stage for them was that of proselyte: this involved circumcision, and the acceptance of further obligations of the Law. There is evidence that the strict Palestinian Jews tried to re-convert the Godfearers of the Dispersion into proselytes of the stricter Jewish Faith.

(3) A man could be freed from an oath sworn *by the Temple* (vv. 16–22), providing that he did not mention the gold on the Temple. In the same way an oath sworn *by the altar* could be broken, providing that there was no mention of the sacrifice upon it. Jesus pointed out that the gold was not sacred apart from the Temple, nor the offering apart from the altar. Neither therefore had any power to strengthen or limit an oath, whether mentioned or not. In effect swearing by the Temple included not only everything in it, but also its owner, God (see Section 50, ex. 3).

(4) The Law required Jews to pay a tithe (vv. 23–24) or tenth part of their harvest (flocks and produce) to God (Leviticus 27$^{30-33}$, Deuteronomy 14^{22}). So careful were the scribes to carry out this obligation with precision that they extended it to tiny herbs. They would carefully strain their wine through muslin, lest there was a gnat in it. That would amount to contact with the dead, and result in ceremonial uncleanness. Such care for detail was commendable, but not when wider duties were

neglected. To strain gnats and, as it were, to swallow camels, was absurd.

(5) Vv. 25–26 compare scribes and Pharisees to cups and dishes washed only on the outside.

(6) It was a custom to whiten graves (vv. 27–28), particularly at festival time, lest pilgrims should make accidental contact with the dead and so become ceremonially disqualified from taking part in the celebrations (cf. Luke 11⁴⁴).

(7) The tombs of many prophets (vv. 29–32) had recently been adorned. But the words can also be taken figuratively: Scribes and Pharisees were quite sure that they would not have treated the prophets as their forefathers had done, but even now they were plotting to kill the one whose coming the prophets had foretold.

For vv. 33–36 see Luke section.

123 · The Widow's Offering   Mark 12⁴¹⁻⁴⁴. Luke 21¹⁻⁴

MARK and LUKE. The incident illustrates Jesus' teaching about alms-giving in the Sermon on the Mount (Matthew 6²⁻⁴). There were thirteen large boxes for almsgiving at the Temple.

124 · On the Mount of Olives   Mark 13. Luke 21⁵⁻³⁸
(17²²⁻³⁷). Matthew 24¹⁻⁵¹

Before studying the chapter the student should have some idea of what scholars mean by the following terms:

Second Advent (Advent from Latin *advenire* – to come). This means the second coming of Jesus in glory.

Parousia (Greek for presence or arrival, especially a royal visit). This terms covers both the second advent and the continuing presence of Christ afterwards. At first the Christian hope was for a visible parousia, but as time passed the idea of a spiritual parousia took its place, which some thought had been fulfilled at Pentecost.

Apocalypse (Greek, corresponding to the Latin 'Revelation'). The terms Apocalypse and Revelation are used to denote an unveiling or revealing of future events. The last book of the Bible has this sort of character, and so is called 'The Revelation', or alternately 'The Apoca-lypse'. Similarly the term is given to any other such writings. Ever since prophets (such as Amos) had foretold a *Day of the Lord* apocalyptic writers had flourished.

Apocalyptic literature often described visions, in which the future was revealed in symbolic language rather than in plain speech. It tended to predict that before the Day of the Lord came God's people would suffer because the powers of evil would have a final outburst. Even nature would react with catastrophes and supernatural signs.

The Old Testament contains some notable examples of apocalyptic writing (e.g. Isaiah 13⁹⁻¹¹, Isaiah 24²¹⁻²³, 25–27, Daniel 7–12, Joel 2, Ezekiel 32⁷⁻¹⁰, Zechariah 9–14). The first Christians also made use of this type of writing, although only one complete Christian apocalypse is included in the New Testament.

Eschatology (from Greek *eschatos* – at the last, finally, the end). The term is used to denote the end of all things, with particular reference to death and judgement. Thus eschatological writing had much in common with apocalyptic.

MARK 13. This chapter is probably based upon a Christian apocalypse, as well as upon actual sayings of Jesus. Which parts belong to Jesus and which to Christian apocalypse, it is impossible to say with certainty, but Jesus, it should be remembered, was a Jew, familiar with apocalyptic thought, and very likely himself a user of apocalyptic language.

The building of Herod's Temple (vv. 1–2) had commenced as far back as 19–20 B.C., but it was not completed until A.D. 62–64, about the time when this Gospel was written. Jesus foretold its destruction, as Micah and Jeremiah had predicted the destruction of Solomon's Temple (Micah 3¹², Jeremiah 26⁶). His words came true in A.D. 70.

Vv. 3–8 are a private revelation to a few – a typical feature of apocalypse. The subject is the second advent and parousia. Mark probably had in mind some known Jewish nationalist leaders, the famine mentioned in Acts 11²⁸, and the earthquake recorded in Acts 16²⁶.

Jesus had often warned his disciples that suffering not only awaited him but could also be expected by them (vv. 9–13, cf. Mark 8³¹⁻³⁸). By the time this Gospel was written, the Christian Faith had spread through most of the Roman Empire, and the first Christian persecution (under Nero) had taken place. The apostles Peter and Paul had been put to death, and Christians in Rome (whence this Gospel originated) needed all the encouragement of this apocalyptic writing. Their sufferings, so Mark implies, were but the prelude to the parousia.

The Abomination of Desolation in vv. 14–27 is described in Daniel as *the abomination that maketh desolate* (Daniel 9²⁷, 11³¹, 12¹¹). It was an altar to Zeus, set up in the Temple by King Antiochus Epiphanes during the Greek invasion of Palestine, 168 B.C. (I Maccabees 1⁵⁴). It is mentioned in Mark probably to predict a similar desecration of the Temple by the Romans, as indeed took place in A.D. 70. An alternative suggestion is that the verse refers to the attempt made in A.D. 38 by the Emperor Caligula to erect a statue to himself in the Temple.

Before the final siege of Jerusalem, the Christians heeded the warning in vv. 15–18 and fled to Pella beyond the Jordan.

V. 19 comes from Daniel 12¹. In vv. 21–22, after signs on earth come supernatural signs in the heavens (cf. Isaiah 13¹⁰, Isaiah 34⁴, Joel 32⁷⁻⁹, Ezekiel 32⁷⁻⁹). Finally comes the second advent and parousia, described in words from Daniel 7¹³ (cf. Jesus' answer in Mark 14⁶², and see Section 139). The angels would help in gathering the *elect*, i.e. Christians from all parts of the world. (For Jews, the *elect* were all Jews dispersed throughout the empire.) The *four winds* are mentioned in Zechariah 2⁶. The *uttermost parts* is an expression from Deuteronomy 13⁷, 30⁴.

In vv. 28–37, the discourse ends with a parable about being observant and a parable about being watchful. *Neither the son* does not occur in some manuscripts, possibly because the phrase suggests a limitation of Jesus' divinity. As a human being, however, his knowledge of such matters was restricted like that of other men.

LUKE. Mark wrote around A.D. 65. Luke wrote around A.D. 80 when the fall of Jerusalem had taken place. So, although he made use of the apocalypse in Mark he made certain modifications. Luke should therefore be compared with Mark, and these differences noted:

Mark 13¹¹ is found in Luke 12¹¹.

Luke 21¹⁹ is a proverbial expression.

In vv. 20–28, Luke speaks precisely of *Jerusalem compassed* and of its *desolation* (instead of the abomination). He can say also, *they . . . shall be led captive into all the nations.* Many Jewish captives were taken to various cities throughout the empire for execution, and, of course, to Rome for the triumph procession of Titus, the general to whom Jerusalem had surrendered.

In v. 24, instead of the second advent coming at the same time as the fall of Jerusalem, as in Mark, there is a period of delay. *The times of the Gentiles* is an idea borrowed from Daniel to mean a period of Gentile oppression.

Luke omits Mark's parable of The Watchful Servants, and instead writes a reminder (vv. 34–36) of the need to be in a fit state *to stand before the Son of man.* He also omits to mention that neither the angels nor the Son know the exact time of the Second Advent.

Vv. 37 and 38 say that Jesus probably camped out on the Mount of Olives, as did many pilgrims. He very likely used the Garden of Gethsemane. Mark says that he spent each evening at Bethany. According to the Fourth Gospel, Bethany was the home of his friends, Mary, Martha and Lazarus.

MATTHEW. Matthew uses Mark 13 as the basis of his apocalypse, but includes some extra material. (The comments for Matthew 24^{1-36} can be found in the Mark section for Chapter 13^{1-32}.)

V. 27 indicates that the parousia will be visible to the entire world. V. 28 is a proverb for something inevitable. (There is a possible connection with the military eagles of Rome). Vv. 37–42 compare the suddenness of the second advent with that of Noah's flood. Vv. 43–44 emphasize this unexpectedness by a short parable.

In vv. 45–51, instead of Mark's short parable about The Watchful Servants, Matthew ends with a more detailed parable about Good and Bad Servants.

125 · Jesus Anointed at Bethany   Mark 14^{1-9}. Matthew 26^{1-13}

Presumably Simon had recovered from his disease, or possibly Jesus had cured him. The Synoptic Gospels do not give the name of the woman. (John 12^3 says that she was Mary, the sister of Martha and Lazarus. It has been suggested that Simon was perhaps their father, or some other close relative. In this Gospel the anointing took place *six days before the Passover*, on the day before the Triumphal Entry.)

Anointing had a three-fold association. Kings were anointed before their coronation (as English sovereigns are); The Messiah was the Anointed of God (Hebrew Messiah = Greek Christ = The Anointed One); Bodies were anointed for burial. Thus anointing was symbolic of kingship, messiahship, and death. It could therefore be that the woman anointed Jesus as an act of homage to him as a King-Messiah, and that Jesus accepted it as a Suffering-Servant Messiah.

The ointment used was costly. A penny or denarius was equal in value to a workman's daily wage. Some manuscripts of Mark say that the disciples were the ones who complained (as does Matthew). John 12^4 mentions Judas in particular. The promise in v. 9 is all the more definite because, by the time that this Gospel was written, the story had been told and re-told for over thirty years.

LUKE 7^{36-50}. Instead of the anointing at Bethany, Luke tells of an earlier anointing at Capernaum. This took place in the house of another Simon, a Pharisee. There are differences and similarities between the stories (see Section 65).

MATTHEW. Matthew closely follows Mark. He says that the disciples were the people who protested at the seeming waste.

126 · Jewish and Roman Reckoning of Days

JEWISH RECKONING OF DAYS
(from Sunset to Sunset)

Thursday Nisan 13th	Friday Nisan 14th	Saturday Nisan 15th	Sunday 1st day of week
Sunset 6 p.m.	Sunset 6 p.m.	Sunset 6 p.m.	Sunset 6 p.m.
	The Last Supper	The Crucifixion	Passover meal eaten	The women return to the tomb at dawn
		The Preparation Passover Lamb sacrificed in the afternoon The body of Jesus taken down from the Cross so that the Sabbath would not be profaned It is buried hastily before sunset First Day of Unleavened Bread	The Sabbath and The Passover also Feast of Unleavened Bread	
Midnight	Midnight	Midnight	Midnight
13th	14th	15th	

ROMAN RECKONING OF DAYS
(from Midnight to Midnight)

114

127 · Judas Betrays Jesus   Mark 14[10-11]. Luke 22[1-6].
                                       Matthew 26[14-16]

Judas' motives and those of the chief priests are discussed in Sections 128 and 129.

LUKE. Luke mentions not only the chief priests but also the captains – the Temple guard or police, who would make the arrest. Luke's comment on Judas' action is, *And Satan entered into Judas. . . .*

MATTHEW. Matthew specifies the amount of money paid. According to the Law, this was the amount payable as compensation for the loss of a slave (Exodus 21[32]) (see section 142).

128 · Why did Judas Betray Jesus?

(1) The Gospel accounts suggest greed (Matthew 26[15], John 12[6]). Even allowing for the fact that the character of Judas in the Gospels is coloured by the feeling that Christians had for him, greed might have been his motive. But he must have been very desperate to have gone to such lengths to achieve it, and the amount paid, according to Matthew, was not very large. It could have been more. Nevertheless great crimes have on occasion been committed for very little gain.

(2) Another suggestion emphasizes ambition. Thus Judas was ambitious for Jesus and for himself. He hoped that Jesus would be the great earthly King-Messiah of popular expectation. This would mean that he, Judas, would hold important office. (The other apostles shared this hope.) But Jesus had missed many splendid opportunities, e.g. after the feeding of the five thousand, and the Triumphal Entry. If only Jesus were delivered into the hands of his enemies, he would have to act. It never occurred to Judas that things might go otherwise.

(3) A third possibility is self-preservation. Judas, seeing that the enemies of Jesus were closing in, went over to the other side.

Any one of these may have been his motive, or possibly a mixture of them all. One thing seems certain: Judas did not hate his master, or wish him greatly to suffer. His remorse proves that.

129 · Why was Judas Employed to Betray Jesus?

(1) The Gospels say that Judas was going to let the chief priests know when Jesus could be found alone. Yet their own spies could have reported that Jesus spent each evening quietly at Bethany.

I   *115*

(2) The Gospels also say that Judas went with the Temple police to identify Jesus. Judas's help, especially among trees, would be useful, but was it essential? Someone else to do this could easily have been found. Apart from the fact that Judas' presence might allay the suspicions of the other apostles until it was too late for them to act, nothing would be gained.

(3) A very reasonable suggestion is that Judas told the chief priests that Jesus had definitely admitted to the Twelve that he was the Messiah. This was the very evidence that his enemies had been seeking. So far there had been no public statement of his that could be quoted in a court of law. Now the high priest could ask Jesus, *Art thou the Christ?*, and be sure of the answer (cf. Mark 14[62-64]). When Judas had supplied this information, he could also be made use of for purposes 1 and 2.

An objection to this theory is that Judas did not appear at the trial as a witness. This, however, is not surprising. Jewish Law required at least two witnesses, and there was no one to corroborate Judas' evidence.

130 · The Preparation for the Supper

Mark 14[12-16].
Luke 22[7-13].
Matthew 26[17-19]

The information in v. 12 (and in the corresponding verses of Luke and Matthew) involves a number of difficulties. They are discussed in Section 132.

Very likely the room used was in the house of John Mark's mother, because that, we are told in Acts 12, was later a regular meeting-place for Jesus' followers. What was more likely than that the house of the Last Supper, which would have many special associations for them, should continue to be so frequented?

Had Jesus given the exact address, Judas could so easily have overheard, and passed on the information. A man carrying a pitcher of water was unusual, because women were the water-carriers, but not sufficiently so as to attract attention. The man may have been John Mark himself, or his father.

LUKE. Luke supplies the information that the two disciples sent were Peter and John.

MATTHEW. Matthew omits the details of the man with the pitcher.

131 · The Last Supper   Mark 14¹⁷⁻²⁶. Luke 22¹⁴⁻³⁸.
                          Matthew 26²⁰⁻³⁰

As they sat in v. 18 means 'as they reclined' on cushions or couches.
The dish was a common dish of herbs and savouries. The statement in
v. 20 was an indirect appeal to the traitor, because it would remind the
Twelve of the words in Psalm 41⁹.

The statement in v. 21 shows that Jesus believed his death to be
indicated in the Scriptures. Although there is no mention in the Scriptures of suffering connected with the Son of man, in Isaiah 53 there is
very definite mention of the Suffering-Servant Messiah. Jesus combined
the ideas of the Son of man and the Suffering Servant.

The blessing in v. 22 was presumably the usual Jewish thanksgiving
over food, as again in v. 23. In speaking of his body and blood separately
Jesus was using sacrificial language, because an important feature of
Jewish sacrifice was the separating of the blood from the victim's body.

Jesus spoke of a New Covenant. The Old Covenant (Testament or
Contract) had been made between God and his people at Mount
Sinai, with the help of Moses (Exodus 24¹⁻⁸). The blood of a sacrifice
was sprinkled by Moses, first upon an altar, as representing God, and
then upon the people. Thus the two contracting parties were bound
together by the blood of the sacrifice.

This covenant failed, because, although God kept his part, the people
broke theirs. Jeremiah said that there would one day have to be made a
new covenant (Jeremiah 31³¹). In the view of the Christian Church this
New Covenant was inaugurated by the blood of Jesus, in the upper
room and on the hill of Calvary. The words *which is shed for many*
allude to Isaiah 53¹².

The part of the Bible that tells of the making and breaking of the Old
Covenant (Testament) is consequently called the Old Testament. The
New Testament is the part that tells of Jesus, and of the making of the
New Covenant between God and the New Israel (that is, the Christian
Church).

This Last Supper shows that Jesus wanted his followers to regard his
death as something far more than mere judicial murder by his enemies,
or high-minded suicide by himself.

V. 25 suggests a parting and later a reunion, between Jesus and his
followers. The first Christians felt that the kingdom mentioned here
was the Christian Church. After the coming of the Holy Spirit on the
Feast of Pentecost, they met together every first day of the week (that is,
on the weekly return of the day of the resurrection) for the 'Breaking of
Bread'. They repeated the words and actions of Jesus at the Last Supper,
and so, in a sort of spiritual parousia, had their master's presence with

them again, until such time as his actual visible parousia should take place.

The *hymn* in v. 26 would be a psalm.

LUKE. Luke alone, in v. 19, has the command *Do this in remembrance of me*. He takes it from the earliest record of the Last Supper, in I Corinthians 11²³⁻²⁵. Some scholars question whether Jesus did give this command, especially as his second advent was expected soon. However, since the early Christians did repeat the words and actions often, it could well be that they had had some such command, and that this command outweighed any expectation of theirs that Jesus would make an early return. In I Corinthians 11²⁵⁻²⁶ the command and the coming are linked.

Whereas Mark begins the supper with mention of the betrayer, Luke puts Jesus' warning about him at the end.

At v. 23 Luke introduces some teaching about humility (cf. Luke 9⁴⁶ and Mark 9³⁴). Vv. 25–26 are taken from Mark 10⁴²⁻⁴⁴. For the feet washing see John 13¹⁻¹⁰. In vv. 29–30 Jesus uses the familiar symbol of a banquet to represent the Messianic kingdom. V. 30 corresponds to Matthew 19²⁸. The warning to Peter, etc. follows here, for Luke places it in the upper room (see Section 134).

MATTHEW. Matthew's account is based on Mark's. As well as mentioning that the disciples asked, *Is it I, Lord?*, he says that Judas separately asked, *Is it I, Rabbi?* and that Jesus replied, *Thou hast said. Unto the remission of sins* in v. 28 is Matthew's own addition.

132 · The Last Supper as a Passover Meal

The Synoptic Gospels state clearly that Jesus sent two disciples to make ready the Passover. The Passover commemorated God's deliverance of the Hebrews from Egyptian slavery (Exodus 12). In the course of time the commemoration acquired a definite ceremonial. It took place in the first month of the year, Abib or Nisan (about our March). On the tenth day each family or household took a male lamb, a year old, and without blemish. On Nisan 14 it was taken to the Temple, and killed during the late afternoon. That same night (by Jewish reckoning now Nisan 15) the lamb was roasted and eaten. The meal had to be held within the boundaries of Jerusalem, which included for this purpose the Mount of Olives. The youngest member of the family asked, 'What mean ye by this service?' The head of the family replied, 'It is the sacrifice of the Lord's Passover . . .'

The day following the meal was the Feast of Unleavened Bread, observed for seven days from Nisan 15–21. This feast was a reminder of the actual escape from Egypt, when, such was the haste, there was no time to wait for bread to rise in the usual way.

So closely connected were the two feasts that the Passover and Unleavened Bread became alternative names for the eight days Nisan 14–21, and Nisan 14 could be referred to as the first day of Unleavened Bread as well as being the day when the Passover lambs were sacrificed (Mark 14^{12}).

Jesus could not have been crucified on Nisan 15, the actual Passover feast day, and that year also a Sabbath, because the chief priests would then have been too occupied in the Temple to take part in the early morning trials, and they had themselves decided to avoid that day (Mark 14^2). On this day also Jewish men would not carry arms (as they did when Jesus was arrested), and no one could have bought linen and spices (Mark 15^{46}, 16^1). The Last Supper therefore must have taken place on the evening beginning Nisan 14 (i.e. our Thursday).

For this reason some scholars question whether the Last Supper was in fact a Passover meal. There are three considerations:

(1) It could be that Jesus anticipated the Passover meal because he was aware of Judas' treachery, and his own imminent danger. The lambs were not then killed, but, since there is no mention of one in the Gospels, Jesus may have decided to hold an incomplete Passover meal. There is no record of the contents of the common dish.

(2) When the Passover coincided with a Sabbath, preparing and eating the Passover meal late on Friday night broke into the Sabbath. Some Jews, therefore, and perhaps Jesus was one, preferred to hold the meal on the Thursday evening. Others said that, since the Passover was more important than the Sabbath, it superseded the Sabbath. In this particular year, therefore, some Jews would eat the Passover on the Thursday night, and some on the Friday.

(3) Pharisees and Sadducees did not agree as to when Nisan precisely began. The Sadducean reckoning was the official calendar, but a concession was made to Pharisees, allowing them to eat the Passover meal a day earlier, and so make up for the calendar discrepancy. In these circumstances, Jesus would be following Pharisaic custom, if he ate the Passover on the Thursday.

The Passover commemorated God's deliverance of his people from captivity in Egypt, but after the death and resurrection of Jesus there was a new Passover for Christians to celebrate – God's deliverance of his people from the captivity of sin. Thus, whether the Last Supper was or was not a Passover meal, it was inevitable and appropriate in Christian thought that the death of Jesus, which took place probably as the lambs were being sacrificed in the Temple, should be linked with the ideas behind the Passover (see John 1^{29}, I Corinthians 5^7, Revelation 5^{12}).

133 · The Last Supper as a Chaburah Meal

If the Last Supper was not a Passover meal, an alternative suggestion is that it was a Chaburah meal, such as was held when a group of friends met together for social and religious fellowship. Usually this was held early on a Friday evening, and was by way of being a preparation for the Sabbath. If the Sabbath happened also to be a feast day, the Chaburah meeting would be held on a Thursday evening, so as not to clash with the eve of the festival.

Some of the reasons for supposing that the Last Supper was a Chaburah are as follows:

(1) A Chaburah was held weekly, and the first Christians met weekly, for the Breaking of Bread, their Communion Service. Had the Last Supper been a normal Passover meal, only an annual commemoration would suggest itself, but I Corinthians 11[23-25] (the earliest record of the Last Supper) presupposes a frequent occurrence.

(2) The words in Luke 22[15], instead of expressing Jesus' relief at his being able to eat the Passover, could mean that his desire to do so was not in fact fulfilled.

(3) The details given of the Last Supper have much in common with a Chaburah meal. For example:

(a) As guests arrived, there would be a solemn washing of hands, and possibly a cup of wine, after the usual thanksgiving, would be handed round (cf. Luke 22[17-18]).

(b) When the meal began, the one presiding would take bread and break it, saying, 'Blessed be thou, O Lord our God, eternal King, who bringest forth bread from the earth'. He would then eat a fragment, and give a piece to each guest. (This could be the point at which Jesus added, *This is my body*.)

(c) As the meal proceeded, each food would be blessed by the host, but wine served would be blessed by each individual as he received it.

(d) At the end of the meal, hands would be washed again. (This perhaps was when John 13[3-12] occurred.)

(e) After any meal a final Grace was said by the one presiding, but at a Chaburah meal the Grace would be more solemnly recited over a cup of wine, called 'the cup of blessing'. Such solemn blessing was known as a Kiddush (a making holy). It would include words of thanksgiving 'for thy covenant which thou hast sealed in our flesh' (cf. Luke 22[20]).

(f) A Chaburah meal would conclude with a psalm (Mark 14[26]).

Crucifixion and Resurrection

134 · On the Way to Gethsemane

Mark 14²⁷⁻³¹. Luke 22³¹⁻³⁸.
Matthew 26³¹⁻³⁵

Gethsemane means Oil Press. Jesus in v. 27 was quoting from Zechariah 13⁷. Cock-crow was the first indication of dawn breaking. Roman soldiers had an official dawn signal given to garrisons on night duty: it was called 'cock crowing'.

LUKE. In Luke's Gospel the warning to Peter is given while he is still in the upper room. Jesus speaks to him first as Simon, as he foretold the temptation to come, and then as Peter, the Rock, as a reminder of the need to stand firm.

In v. 35 Jesus reminds the disciples of the time when he sent them on a missionary tour in Galilee. Then they were dependent upon the generosity of others. Now (v. 36) they must be prepared to look after themselves. V. 37 is a quotation from Isaiah 53¹², showing once again that the Fourth Servant Song was in Jesus' thoughts.

The command to buy a sword has been interpreted by some to mean that Jesus contemplated armed resistance. This is unlikely, for Jesus rebuked the one who drew a sword (Matthew 26⁵²), and the first Christians were noted for their non-resistance. It is far more likely that the sword is symbolical of the need to be ready for any danger. *It is enough* suggests that the disciples had not seen its meaning.

MATTHEW. Matthew's account is taken from Mark.

135 · In the Garden of Gethsemane

Mark 14³²⁻⁴².
Luke 22³⁹⁻⁴⁶.
Matthew 26³⁶⁻⁴⁶

V. 34 makes allusion to Psalm 88³⁻⁴. *Abba* is Aramaic for Father. *Cup* is symbolic of suffering (10³⁹). V. 42 means going forward to meet the people approaching.

There are some interesting points of comparison between this incident and the transfiguration. There is the same sense of vision and revelation. On Mount Hermon, Peter, James and John had seen Jesus' divinity: in the Garden the same three see his humanity. In each story Jesus was parted a little distance away; in each the three fell into a trance-like sleep; in each, as they awoke, they *wist not what to answer* (cf. Luke 9³² and Mark 9⁶).

LUKE. Luke's account is very different from Mark's. There is no mention of the Garden, or that Peter, James and John were singled out. There is no repeated prayer: Jesus calmly kneels to pray, and then returns.

The mention in Luke of the angel and the sweat of blood may be additions to his original story. They are somewhat out of keeping with the tone of the Gospel, in which Luke omits or softens much of the tragedy; the verses in which they are mentioned are absent from some important manuscripts; and, if they are omitted, vv. 42 and 45 join together more easily. On the other hand, Luke could have had a professional interest in physical reactions. A sweat of blood, though rare, is not unknown to medical men in cases of extreme mental anguish. And as angels were present in the wilderness (Mark 1¹³) so a ministering angel could well have been present at this later onslaught of temptation.

MATTHEW. Matthew closely follows Mark, but adds the words of the second prayer, v. 42.

136 · The Arrest

Mark 14⁴³⁻⁵². Luke 22⁴⁷⁻⁵³. Matthew 26⁴⁷⁻⁵⁶

A kiss (v. 44) was a customary courtesy (Luke 7⁴⁵). V. 45 R.V. margin reads, *kissed him much.* The Fourth Gospel says that it was Peter referred to in v. 51, and that the servant's name was Malchus (John 18¹⁰, ¹¹).

The mysterious young man in vv. 51–52 is mentioned only here. If he had nothing to do with the arrest, this would be pointless. So a likely explanation is that he was John Mark himself. If the Last Supper was indeed held at his mother's house, then Judas possibly led the soldiers there first. John Mark, having gone to bed, but realizing that Jesus was in danger, would rush to the Garden to warn him.

LUKE. Luke's account is partly from Mark, but there are differences. V. 48 suggests that Judas did not actually kiss Jesus. There is no mention either that a kiss was a sign pre-arranged. Luke says that it was one of two disciples who began to use his sword, but does not say which. (V. 38 states that the apostles had with them two swords.) John 18¹⁰, ¹¹ gives further information. It is Luke only who says (by way of medical interest perhaps) that Jesus healed the wounded man.

To Jesus' words about his being arrested as though he were a dangerous criminal, Luke adds, *but this is your hour, and the power of darkness.* Night was the time appropriate to evil deeds. Luke does not mention that the disciples deserted Jesus.

MATTHEW. Matthew adds to Mark's account some information of his own. When Judas kissed Jesus, Jesus said, *Friend, do that for which thou art come* (v. 52). Jesus rebuked the disciple using the sword, saying that those who resort to violence may expect violence in return.

137 · The Jewish Trials

Although the two occasions when Jesus was brought before the Sanhedrin are referred to as 'trials', the term is used only for convenience. They were not proper legal trials according to Jewish Law, and under Roman rule it is unlikely that the Sanhedrin could hold a capital trial without Roman permission first being obtained. According to the Fourth Gospel, the Roman Governor was willing for this to happen after he himself had actually met the prisoner (John 18³¹).

The Jewish trials were really a night-time questioning to see whether a case could be made, and a short morning consultation of the Sanhedrin at which the case against the prisoner was given official approval, and made ready for presentation to the Governor. Thus the only trial in the strict sense was the Roman one.

Even had the high priest and Sanhedrin previously obtained permission to hold a formal trial, they made little attempt to keep their own rules. For example:

(1) It was illegal to hold a trial at night or on the eve of a feast.

(2) Capital trials had to begin and end during day-time. A trial had to be adjourned to a second day, if it was likely that a prisoner would be found guilty.

(3) Sentence could not be executed on the same day as the trial.

(4) Disagreement between witnesses put an end to a trial.

(5) False witnesses were liable to the punishment prescribed for the offence alleged.

(6) A prisoner was not to be condemned on his own admission.

138 · The Six Trials (summary)

1. *Before Annas.* A preliminary interrogation by the father-in-law of the high priest, Caiaphas (John 18$^{12-14, \; 19-24}$).

2. *Before Caiaphas,* and such members of the Sanhedrin as were available. A preliminary hearing of the case (Mark 14$^{53-65}$, Matthew 26$^{59-68}$). The occasion of Peter's denials.

3. *Before the whole Sanhedrin* at daybreak. To give official approval to the sentence already passed (Mark 15^1, Luke 22$^{66-71}$, Matthew 27^1).

4. *Before Pilate* (Mark 15$^{1-20}$, Matthew 27$^{11-31}$, Luke 23$^{1-7}$, John 18^{28}–19^{16}).

5. *Before Herod* (Luke 23$^{8-12}$).

6. *Before Pilate again* (Luke 23$^{13-25}$).

139 · The Trial before the High Priest and Sanhedrin

Mark 14$^{53-65}$.
Matthew 26 $^{57-68}$

It is unlikely that the full Sanhedrin of seventy members, and the required witnesses, were present at such short notice, but, since the arrest was anticipated, the minimum number of twenty-three members had probably been summoned to attend this emergency meeting (v. 53).

Jewish Law required the agreement of at least two witnesses (Deuteronomy 17^6, 19^{15}). Each witness was solemnly warned that if he gave false witness in a trial for life, blame for the death of the accused would rest upon the witness. On this occasion the warning was a mere formality: the witnesses were called expressly because they were false (v. 57).

A threat to the Temple was blasphemy (v. 58). The subject matter of this evidence was later used to mock Jesus (15^{29}).

Did Jesus ever say, *I will destroy this temple,* or *I am able to destroy the temple* (Matthew 26^{61})? Evidently he had on some occasion spoken about the Temple. The Fourth Gospel records Jesus as saying, *Destroy this temple, and in three days I will raise it up* (John 2^{19}). John's words are more likely to be near the truth than the evidence of the false witnesses, and there is much difference between *I will destroy,* and *Destroy* in the imperative, meaning 'You destroy'. Jesus was possibly foretelling the destruction of the Temple by the Romans.

For the first Christians these words would mean that the Christian Faith had taken the place of the Jewish Faith, of which the Temple was the outward sign. It may well have been that the original saying of Jesus inspired Stephen's words in Acts 7^{48}, and Paul's in Acts 17^{24}. The Fourth Gospel has its own explanation (John 2$^{21-22}$).

With the silence of Jesus in v. 61 compare Isaiah 53[7]. Jesus knew that defence was useless because his enemies had already decided their verdict. To the question, *Art thou the Christ?* however, he could not now remain silent. Possibly Caiaphas had already learned from Judas what the incriminating answer would be. Jesus not only said, *I am*, but added Messianic words from Psalm 110[1] and Daniel 7[13].

Caiaphas, secretly delighted, tore his garments in a show of horror (cf. II Kings 19[1]). It was the custom to cover the face of a condemned criminal (Esther 7[8]), and, since this particular prisoner claimed to be a prophet, his guards tried to make him prophesy.

MATTHEW. Matthew closely follows Mark, but with a few additions. Where Mark says, *the whole council sought witness* (14[55]), Matthew says, *the whole council sought false witness*. The false witnesses, it appears, had official encouragement. In Matthew, the high priest's question is framed as a solemn oath, and Jesus' answer is not the plain *I am* but *Thou hast said* (cf. also Luke 22[70]).

This reply has received various interpretations, thus:

(1) As it is recorded, no precise meaning can be attached to it (least of all that Jesus thereby claimed, or openly admitted, his Messiahship).

(2) Jesus deliberately answered vaguely, feeling that nothing was to be gained now by attempting to distinguish between his idea of Messiahship and the Sanhedrin's.

(3) Such a phrase, according to Jewish use (and sometimes ours) definitely meant 'Yes'. That was certainly how the Sanhedrin chose to regard it.

Matthew does not mention that Jesus was blindfolded, perhaps because such a procedure was well known to Jewish Christians, but this is implied by the servants' wanting Jesus to guess who struck him.

140 · Peter's Denials

Mark 14[54, 66–72]. Luke 22[54–62]. Matthew 26[58, 69–75]

The recognition in vv. 67 and 69 imply that Jesus and the Twelve were well known in Jerusalem. (In a number of manuscripts of Mark's Gospel there is no mention of a cock crowing at this point.) The guesswork in v. 70 was based on Peter's northern intonation.

LUKE. Luke's story is probably based upon Mark's, but makes no mention of the night-time questioning, and adds several touches of its own. In v. 56 Peter is recognized in the *light of the fire*. The second questioner is a man, and his third also.

Luke omits that Peter began to curse, but implies this by saying that *the Lord turned, and looked* upon him, perhaps having heard the voice as he was conducted past.

MATTHEW. Matthew's account is taken from Mark's, but he does not mention the fire, and makes the second questioner another maid.

141 · The Questioning at Daybreak

Mark 15¹. Luke 22⁶³⁻⁷¹. Matthew 27¹⁻²

This trial took place at about six o'clock in the morning. The Roman Governor was not likely to be interested in a charge of blasphemy, but a person claiming to be the Messiah (or, in Greek, Christ) was a person claiming to be a king. So such a claim could be presented as treason against the Roman State.

Actually the Jews themselves were not over concerned with Jesus' possible blasphemy: the possibility of treason alarmed them more. The high priest and Sanhedrin had been allowed considerable freedom of worship and rule by the Romans. All this would be lost if Rome thought that a popular Messianic movement had their encouragement. In the Fourth Gospel this situation is expressed by Caiaphas himself (John 11⁴⁷⁻⁵⁰).

LUKE. According to Luke this is the first and only Jewish trial. Nevertheless its details are almost a repetition of the night-questioning as recorded by Mark and Matthew, and a hint is given that this had taken place. Thus Luke mentions, before the morning trial, the blindfolding of Jesus (a sign of his condemnation), and the attempts to make him prophesy, which Mark and Matthew put after the night-questioning (Luke 22⁶³⁻⁶⁵).

MATTHEW. Matthew is almost the same as Mark.

142 · The Death of Judas

Matthew 27³⁻¹⁰

Matthew's is the only Gospel to make mention of the suicide of Judas Iscariot. There is, however, a mention of it in Acts 1¹⁶⁻²⁰. In Acts it is said that Judas himself bought a field. Evidently by the time that these two accounts were written there existed in Jerusalem a burial place known as *the Field of Blood*, or Akeldama, which Christian tradition associated in some way with Judas.

The words quoted in v. 9 are abridged from Zechariah 11¹²⁻¹³, and not from Jeremiah, as Matthew states. In Zechariah the passage follows one in which the prophet has assumed the part of a shepherd to the people of Israel. In the passage quoted, the prophet thinks of himself as being paid for his work. Sarcastically he says that he is given *the goodly price* of a mere thirty pieces of silver. This he feels moved to throw away in contempt, either to a potter, or into the treasury of the Temple. The latter is more likely, because of the similarity in Hebrew between the word for potter (*yaser*) and the word for treasury (*osar*), and the fact that the casting away was *in the house of the Lord.*

In the money paid to Judas, and the disposal of it, Matthew saw these words were fulfilled. Judas, like the prophet, received his payment for his work; Judas, like the prophet, found no satisfaction in the payment; Judas, like the prophet, threw the money away in the Temple; a potter, or his field, comes into both stories.

Mark does not mention the precise amount. So some scholars consider that Matthew put it at thirty pieces of silver so as to fit his quotation, but the amount could have been as he states, for that, being the price of a slave, was the sort of round sum that he might be offered.

The reason for Matthew's confusing Zechariah with Jeremiah is that in Jeremiah also there is mention of a potter and a field (Jeremiah 18^2, 32^9).

143 · The Roman Trial

Mark 15^{1-20}. Luke 23^{1-25}. Matthew 27^{11-31}

As soon as the case against Jesus had been made ready by the Sanhedrin, he was taken to the Roman governor, for the Jewish sentence to be confirmed on the grounds of treason. Pilate addressed Jesus as King of the Jews, because the chief priests were pressing that point. The *many things* in Mark 15^4 were presumably instances of alleged treasonable activities. *Envy* means ill-will.

Compared with the scheming chief priests, the character of Pilate as shown in the Gospels is much the more favourable. The Jewish King Agrippa I, a contemporary, described him as 'obstinate and merciless', but Jews were not likely to have anything good to say about a Roman procurator. Christians, on the other hand, were more concerned to show in their writing that the Jews were more responsible for the death of their Messiah, and the persecution of his followers, than were the Romans. As the Gospel accounts of Jesus' trial were written after persecution by the Romans had begun, it would not have been wise to lay overmuch blame on the Roman authority.

Even so, Pilate doubtless did want to save Jesus if possible because:

(1) He was responsible for the administration of Roman justice, and there was no evidence that Jesus was likely to be a danger to Rome.

(2) He possibly thought that it was particularly unpleasant when a conquered nation was prepared to hand a fellow-countryman over to the enemy power.

(3) He knew from personal experience what it was like to be out of favour with the chief priests, and possibly felt some sympathy with the prisoner on this account.

When Pilate had first arrived in Palestine as governor he had offended the chief priests by erecting on the ramparts of the Tower of Antonia, overlooking the Temple, imperial standards bearing the Emperor's image. The action was regarded by all devout Jews as sacrilege. Pilate had thought that there was nothing that they could do but submit, for they dared not attack the Roman fortress where the standards were displayed. In a short time, however, some five thousand unarmed Jews had surrounded his headquarters at Caesarea, sixty miles away, in silent protest. To disperse so many by force could not be done by a man who wished to prove to his superiors his competence as a newly appointed governor. So Pilate ordered the removal of the standards.

(4) Perhaps in protecting the prisoner the governor would soothe this and other hurts that his pride had suffered.

To release at festival times a prisoner whom the people might name was a concession not unheard of in ancient times. The custom at Jerusalem may have been established by Pilate himself. The crowd favoured Barabbas possibly as a local hero, a popular rebel, and a quasi-Messiah. The main part had probably assembled to ask for him. The chief priests took advantage of this.

There is evidence in a number of ancient manuscripts that Barabbas also was named Jesus (a not uncommon name) but Christians disliked the coincidence, and substituted *one called Barabbas*. Barabbas itself means 'son of a father', and was possibly a nickname, or a pseudonym assumed to cover a distinguished parentage. To distinguish between the prisoners, Pilate had to refer to one as Barabbas, and to the other as the King of the Jews (cf. Matthew 27^{17}).

It would seem that the crowd demanded the death of Jesus because (1) it included supporters of Barabbas, resentful of Pilate's attempted evasion, (2) mob hysteria swayed the indifferent, (3) the Council had acted too swiftly for many Galilean pilgrims to be present.

Pilate was probably afraid that an unfavourable report of himself would be sent to Rome (John 19^{12}). His record, to which could be added a massacre mentioned in Luke 13^1, was already known there.

The Praetorium was the Governor's residence, and here means the soldiers' own quarters. The *whole band* means also those off duty. Royal purple mocked any claims to kingship. The crown of thorns was a substitute for the laurel wreath worn by Emperors and triumphant generals. The reed served as a sceptre.

LUKE. Luke in v. 2 sets out the charges against Jesus: they add up to one of sedition.

Luke alone gives the trial before Herod Antipas. He could not take the matter out of Pilate's hands completely, because Galilee and Antipas were subject ultimately to the jurisdiction of the Governor, but the King could perhaps share the responsibility of a decision.

The same Herod had killed John the Baptist. He thought that Jesus might be John returned to life, and for a long time had been watching for him in Galilee. He had heard of his miracles, and hoped for a demonstration.

Luke mentions the mockery of Jesus by the soldiers of Herod in place of that by the Roman soldiers (Mark 15[16-20]) and he mentions Barabbas only after the return.

MATTHEW. Matthew's account is much the same as Mark's, with two notable additions:

(1) Pilate's wife's dream (v. 19). According to the apocryphal Gospel of Nicodemus her name was Claudia Procula. Matthew alone mentions the incident. Some scholars say that it may be a legend, perhaps but another instance of the way in which the early Christians blamed the Jews rather than the Romans. Other scholars say that the incident is not improbable, and instance the wife of Julius Caesar. It was certainly not unknown for wives of officials to intervene in matters of justice.

(2) Pilate washed his hands (vv. 24-25). This dramatic action is thought by most scholars to be rather unlikely. Pilate had great need to withdraw from his predicament, but would a Roman governor so publicly admit his inadequacy. Possibly this is another example of the author's anti-Jewish feeling. He was writing for Jewish Christians familiar with the action of hand-washing as a remission of guilt (Deuteronomy 21[1-7]).

The last four words in v. 22 were possibly intended to distinguish between Jesus and another Jesus *called Barabbas*, (see Mark notes).

V. 28 mentions a scarlet robe, whereas Mark has purple. Probably a soldier's red cloak was taken to represent Caesar's imperial purple (and purple has many shades).

144 · The Way to the Cross
Mark 15²⁰⁻²¹. Luke 23²⁶⁻³².
Matthew 27³¹⁻³²

Condemned men had to carry the cross-beams of their crosses. Simon presumably was an African (which was perhaps the reason why the Romans picked him out), but he could have been a colonial Jew. Perhaps he was on his way to the Temple, or, if somebody's servant or slave, returning from some task or duty.

Mark alone mentions Simon's sons, possibly because they became well-known members of the Christian Church in Rome (Romans 16¹³).

LUKE. The two criminals were possibly accomplices of Barabbas.

Luke's special contribution is his mention of the weeping women. Jesus once again predicted the great suffering that would shortly come. The childless would then seem to be the more fortunate. He quoted from Hosea 10⁸, and added a proverb, meaning, 'if they do these things to me, the innocent, what will be the fate of the guilty!' Or, thinking still of the general sufferings, 'if they (the Romans) do these things (i.e. crucify Jews, including one innocent one) while the nation is yet living, what will be, by comparison, the suffering inflicted on Jews when the nation comes to be destroyed' (cf. Mark 11¹²⁻¹⁴, ²⁰⁻²¹).

MATTHEW. Matthew mentions Simon of Cyrene, but not his sons.

145 · The Last Words of Jesus (summary)

1. *Father, forgive them: for they know not what they do* (Luke 23³⁴).

2. *Verily I say unto thee, To-day shalt thou be with me in Paradise* (Luke 23⁴³).

3. *Woman, behold, thy son! . . . Behold, thy mother!* (John 19²⁷).

4. *My God, my God, why hast thou forsaken me?* (Mark 15³⁴; Matthew 27⁴⁶).

5. *I thirst* (John 19²⁸).

6. *It is finished* (John 19³⁰).

7. *Father, into thy hands I commend my spirit* (Luke 23⁴⁶).

146 · The Crucifixion
Mark 15²²⁻⁴¹. Luke 23³³⁻⁴⁹.
Matthew 27³³⁻⁵⁶

The Roman place of execution lay just outside the city wall. It was called Golgotha by the Jews but Calvary by the Romans. Both names mean *the place of the skull,* perhaps because of its shape or use. V. 25 makes the time 9 a.m.

V. 23 refers to a drink of drugged wine, provided out of pity by some Jerusalem women, and permitted by the Romans for prisoners before crucifixion. The merciful custom was prompted also by Scripture (Proverbs 31⁶). Jesus would not drink this wine: he was about to perform his final act as the Suffering Servant, and would not avoid anything that that involved.

In the title on the cross, Pilate managed to have the last say (John 19²²). V. 28 (R.V. margin) quotes from the Fourth Servant Song (Isaiah 53¹²). In v. 29 the passers-by take up the alleged threat to the Temple: to them perhaps it was the one thing that meant anything. To come down from the cross was a repetition of the temptation in the wilderness to do something spectacular.

The darkness in v. 33 was no normal eclipse of the sun: that was impossible at Passover full moon. According to Matthew 27⁵¹ it was the prelude to an earthquake. Whatever the cause, the darkness was appropriate, and to the disciples seemed significant. The sixth to ninth hour would be from noon to 3 o'clock.

The cry in 15³⁴ was in Aramaic, and quoted Psalm 22¹. How far Jesus was, or felt himself to be, forsaken, no one knows, but it should be noted that R.V. margin permits the past tense, and that the psalm as a whole is more one of triumph than of despair. Jesus no doubt found it a source of strength. The evangelist had the psalm in mind when mentioning the parting of his garments (v. 24), and the mockery by the passers-by (v. 29).

The misunderstanding of Jesus' cry in v. 35 presents a difficulty. Elijah was regarded not only as the herald of the Messiah, but as a source of help in time of trouble. It is said that Jews, on hearing the cry to God, would not be likely to mistake that for an appeal to Elijah. Since, however, 'God is the Lord' is the meaning of the name Elijah, the similarity of sound may well have caused confusion. Alternatively, the bystanders may have misunderstood Jesus' words deliberately in order to mock him. Those standing near the cross, however, were mainly Roman soldiers, and they were not likely to know anything about Elijah. In view of the darkness, it is likely that they thought that the call was to Helios, the Greek Sun-god.

The vinegar in v. 36 was sour wine brought by the soldiers as part of their day's rations; the sponge would be a jar-stopper. But who it was who ran, and who said *Let be* is not clear.

(1) He could have been one of the soldiers, moved by pity, and the words *Let be* could have been spoken to his comrades or the by-standers as they tried to stop him. On the other hand, he could have been moved

simply by a desire to keep Jesus alive, so that some supernatural intervention could have a chance to occur. In the former case he would be concocting an excuse for his action on the spur of the moment. In the latter case he would be giving his real reason, only by Elijah he would mean Helios.

(2) He could have been some Jewish bystander, also moved by pity, or anxious to keep Jesus alive. He too would be speaking either to protesting soldiers (whose wine he had taken) or protesting bystanders, and giving similar reasons.

Matthew 27⁴⁸⁻⁴⁹ (also indefinite as to who ran) gives the impression that the act was one of pity. There it is *the rest* who say *Let be*, apparently because they had no wish for such human intervention when something supernatural might occur.

There were two great veils or curtains in the Temple, one at the entrance to the Holy Place, and one screening the Holy of Holies. This latter is the one more probably meant in v. 38. Just as many regard the darkness as symbolical rather than actual, because of words in Scripture about the impending Day of the Lord (e.g. Amos 8⁹) so here the rending of the Temple veil is often interpreted as a symbolic way of saying that Christ's death had both put an end to Judaism and also destroyed the barrier between man and God (cf. Hebrews 10¹⁹⁻²⁰).

In v. 39 R.V. margin permits *a son of God.*

LUKE. Luke alone (v. 34) records Jesus' prayer for those who crucified him. In v. 36 Luke mentions that the soldiers joined in the mockery, offering Jesus their wine (but this would seem to be a variation of Mark 15²³). There is no mention in Luke of mockery by the people. Whereas Mark says briefly that those crucified with Jesus reproached him, Luke gives special details of their words (vv. 39–43).

Luke's also is the only Gospel to record (v. 46) Jesus' dying prayer. The words come from Psalms 31⁵, and show that the stress behind Mark 15³⁴ had passed.

The centurion in Luke (v. 47) speaks of *a righteous man*, instead of *the Son of God* (or *a son*) as in Mark. The reason for the alteration is perhaps that Mark's phrase from the lips of a Roman might suggest to Luke's Gentile readers just another pagan myth about gods appearing in human form, or be thought to refer to the Emperor who was called 'Son of God'.

MATTHEW. Matthew for the most part follows Mark, except for vv. 15–53. It seems that as Jesus died there was a severe earthquake, which caused rocks and rock tombs to be split open. Also about this time, strange stories about visions of departed spirits began to be circulated in Jerusalem. Matthew says that the visions were seen after Jesus' resurrection, because Jesus, of course, was the first to rise again after death (I Corinthians 15²⁰).

According to Christian belief, after Jesus' death *he went and preached unto the spirits in prison* (I Peter 3¹⁹), that is, the departed, so as to convey to them the blessings of his triumph. Matthew therefore probably regarded the visions seen in Jerusalem *of the saints that had fallen asleep* as indication that Christ's victory over death was taking effect already.

Other points of variation in Matthew are:

(1) He does not mention the sons of Simon of Cyrene: their names were of particular interest only to Mark's readers.

(2) The wine offered to Jesus was *mingled with gall*, and not with myrrh, as in Mark. Matthew had in mind Psalm 69²⁰⁻²¹.

(3) The title on the cross bore Jesus' name.

(4) To the words of mockery are added *Son of God* in vv. 40 and 43. This is not merely because the story is told by a Christian. At his trial Jesus had been asked whether he was the Christ of God. In addition to having in mind Psalm 22⁷⁻⁸ when writing of the mockery, as have Mark and Luke, Matthew may also have been thinking of Wisdom 2¹⁷⁻²⁰.

(5) Jesus' cry in v. 46 is quoted in Hebrew, instead of Aramaic as in Mark. It is *the rest* and not the bystanders who gave Jesus a drink, and who said *Let be*.

147 · The Burial

Mark 15⁴²⁻⁴⁷. Luke 23⁵⁰⁻⁵⁶
Matthew 27⁵⁷⁻⁶¹

Romans usually left bodies on crosses to rot away. This was an offence against Jewish Law, so, as a concession to Jewish feelings, the Romans in Palestine took bodies down and buried them in a common grave. This would have happened to the body of Jesus but for Joseph of Arimathaea, possibly a member of the Sanhedrin, for he is described as a *councillor*. The bodies of people crucified were Roman property, but sometimes permission to bury them would be given to relatives or friends.

Pilate was surprised that Jesus should be already dead, because it was not unusual for those crucified to linger on for some days until they died of hunger and exhaustion. The women noted where the body was laid, so that, when the sabbath was past, they could return, and complete the burial ceremonies.

LUKE. Luke gives more information about Joseph, who must have risked the severe displeasure of his fellow-councillors, and possibly his place on the Sanhedrin. Luke states that the tomb had not been used previously.

MATTHEW. Matthew describes Joseph as a rich man (which could account for his influence with Pilate, and his ownership of a private vault) and maybe had in mind Isaiah 53⁹. Matthew says also that Joseph was a disciple.

148 · The Guarding of the Tomb — Matthew 27⁶²⁻⁶⁶

This story is one of Matthew's own special contributions. It presents some problems.

It seems unlikely that the chief priests would anticipate, either that Jesus would rise from the dead, or that an attempt would be made to make it appear that he had. Even the disciples did not anticipate any such thing. Jesus' mentions of rising again had been made only to the Twelve. The chief priests had heard the evidence at the trial, about destroying the Temple, and building it in three days, but would they have interpreted this as a hint from Jesus about his forthcoming resurrection? They themselves knew how the evidence had been manipulated.

On the other hand, since Jesus had claimed to be the Messiah, they could have feared some attempt by his disciples in some way to suggest his immortality. In such case a guard would be a wise precaution.

Scholars incline to the view that the story is the result of some arguments between Christians and Jews, the Jews accusing Christians of having stolen the body, and the Christians pointing out that this they could not have done, because of a guard on duty. There is, however, in the New Testament no trace that any such accusation ever was made in Palestine, and some such trace one might expect, had such an allegation ever been circulated (see Matthew 28¹¹⁻¹⁵).

149 · The Empty Tomb — Mark 16 ¹⁻⁸. Luke 24¹⁻¹¹. Matthew 28¹⁻¹⁵

At sunset on Saturday the Sabbath ended, and shops re-opened. So the women could buy spices for early next day.

Most scholars are agreed that v. 8 is the end of Mark's Gospel. It finishes abruptly, possibly in the middle of a sentence, which, had it been completed, might have said who or what caused the women to be afraid, other than the words that they heard. The remaining verses are an attempt by another writer to complete the Gospel (see Section 151).

LUKE. In Luke *two men stood by them* instead of the one young man mentioned by Mark. Luke makes it clear that they were angels, and gives in greater detail, but with some alteration, Mark's words about going into Galilee. Mark's Gospel does not go on to mention any meeting in Galilee. Presumably none of Luke's other sources mentioned one either, for he also does not include one in his Gospel. Instead, since the promise to meet the disciples in Galilee seemed to Luke to have been unfulfilled, he recalls that it was in Galilee that Jesus first warned the disciples about his coming death.

Mark does not say whether the women did in fact give the message to the disciples and Peter. Luke, however, says that they did, but that their words were taken as nonsense.

MATTHEW. Matthew's account is more dramatic than any other. He tells of an earthquake, and of the rolling away of the stone, and he alone says that as the women went away Jesus met them.

Scholars sometimes explain this incident as being either a variation of the appearance of the risen Jesus to Mary Magdalene (John 20[11–18]), or else a repetition of the incident just mentioned by Matthew, an appearance of the risen Jesus being confused with the appearance of an angel. The message attributed to Jesus is but a shortened form of that given to the women by the angel.

The incident in vv. 11–15, together with the request for a guard to be placed at the tomb, is thought by some scholars to belong to arguments between Jews and Christians. If Christians asserted that the body of Jesus could not have been stolen because some soldiers were on guard, there arose the difficulty of explaining why the soldiers kept quiet about what really happened. This incident gave an explanation: first the soldiers were stunned by the earthquake, and then they were given money to spread a false rumour.

150 · Peter Visits the Tomb   Luke 24[12]

Luke makes only brief mention of Peter's visit to the tomb. The full story is told in the Fourth Gospel (John 20[3–10]).

151 · The Ending of St. Mark's Gospel   Mark 16[9–20]

Reasons for supposing this to be an attempt, by some other person, to finish the Gospel, are:

135

(1) V. 9 introduces Mary Magdalene, yet she has already been mentioned in v. 1.

(2) Scholars say that in the Greek text the style and phrasing are different from those of Mark.

(3) In many ancient and important manuscripts these verses do not occur. It is thought that they originate not later than A.D. 150, since the first mention of them can be traced to that time.

(4) In some ancient manuscripts an alternative, but shorter ending, is given in place of this one.

As the Gospel ends so abruptly, the question arises: Why? One possibility is that persecution interrupted the author. Another possibility is that the ending written by Mark got torn away and lost. This lost ending would probably have contained details of resurrection appearances of Jesus, possibly in Galilee, and possibly to Peter, since the angel at the tomb made special reference to Galilee and Peter.

The Contents of Mark 16⁹⁻²⁰

Vv. 9–11 mention briefly the visit of Mary Magdalene, fully recorded in Luke 24¹⁻¹¹, and the appearance of Jesus to her, fully recorded in John 20¹¹⁻¹⁸.

Vv. 12–13 refer to the appearance of Jesus to two disciples as they went to Emmaus (Luke 24¹³⁻³⁵).

V. 14 briefly mentions the appearance of Jesus to the Eleven in the evening of Easter Day (Luke 24³⁶⁻⁴³).

V. 15 is based on Matthew 28¹⁹.

V. 16 probably refers to the attitude of the Early Church towards non-believers.

Instances of laying hands on the sick, and of casting out devils, in the name of Jesus (vv. 17–18), are numerous, e.g. Acts 16¹⁶⁻¹⁸. Speaking with new tongues was a frequent phenomenon in the Early Church. It marked the outpouring of the Holy Spirit at Pentecost (Acts 2⁴), and upon the newly-converted (Acts 10⁴⁶), and was at times a special gift to believers (I Corinthians 12¹⁰, 14¹⁻¹⁹).

They shall take up serpents refers probably to the incident concerning St. Paul in Acts 28¹⁻⁶.

There is no mention in the New Testament of anyone's drinking poison without harm; but there is early Christian record of this happening to Justus Barsabbas (named in Acts 1²³), and a later tradition that it happened to John the apostle. In art the apostle is sometimes shown holding a poisoned cup.

V. 19 is based upon Acts 1⁹⁻¹¹ and 2³³.

152 · The Walk to Emmaus Luke 24¹³⁻³⁵

This resurrection appearance is referred to in Mark 16¹²⁻¹³, but the story itself is only in Luke. The two disciples were other than the Twelve; probably they were Judaean disciples going back home after attending the Passover. They could have been husband and wife. The site of Emmaus is not known, but it lay about seven and a half miles from Jerusalem.

Their eyes were holden perhaps for natural causes: they were preoccupied; they would not peer closely under the traveller's headscarf; they were not expecting to meet someone whom they supposed to be dead.

The newcomer's questions were answered somewhat impatiently (and cautiously – a possible spy?) but soon the disciples eagerly interrupted each other (vv. 21–24). V. 24 refers to Peter and John (Luke 24¹², John 20³⁻¹⁰). Vv. 25–26 express the truth about the Suffering-Servant Messiah that the Twelve had found so difficult to grasp.

In v. 30 the guest says the usual blessing. The words and the actions were commonplace, the voice apparently still unrecognized, but the upraised hands would reveal nail-marks.

V. 34 refers presumably to the appearance recorded in I Corinthians 15⁵. In v. 35 Luke was very likely thinking of the Christian Communion Service, first known as the Breaking of Bread, and of how the supper at Emmaus had resembled it.

153 · The Evening of Easter Day Luke 24³⁶⁻⁴⁶

This appearance of Jesus to his apostles is referred to in Mark 16¹⁴, which says that they were having their evening meal. The Fourth Gospel says that Thomas was missing on this occasion (John 20²⁴). *Peace be unto you* was the usual Jewish greeting.

Luke's phrase *flesh and bones* may sound somewhat too much like the description of an ordinary human body, but the point that he is trying to make is that Jesus definitely had a body. It was the same body as before, but yet different.

154 · A Mountain in Galilee Matthew 28¹⁶⁻²⁰

The resurrection appearances mentioned by Luke all took place in and around Jerusalem. Matthew (and John) mentions an appearance in

Galilee. The angel at the tomb had told the women that Jesus would meet his disciples, most of whom were Galileans, in Galilee. St. Paul mentions an appearance of the risen Jesus to more than five hundred disciples at once (I Corinthians 15⁶). This is probably the one described by Matthew.

The mountain was evidently a pre-arranged meeting-place. *Some doubted* because, like the apostle Thomas (John 20²⁴⁻²⁹), they were not prepared to be hasty in believing that Jesus was alive.

Jesus first addressed the Eleven in particular, recalling Daniel 7¹⁴. Then followed the great commission to all, to make disciples and baptize converts, *into the name of the Father and of the Son and of the Holy Ghost*. At the time when these words were written the phrase *into the name* meant 'into the ownership'. Thus the Christian convert at baptism became the possession of Father, Son, and Holy Ghost.

In the Acts the first converts are said to have been baptized *into the name of the Lord Jesus* (cf. 2³⁸, 8¹⁶, 10⁴⁸). Apparently this was the original practice, but by the time this Gospel was written the recognized formula had become Father, Son, and Holy Ghost.

The world-wide mission of the Church was one that the first Christians were slow to grasp. Many regarded Christianity as only the fulfilment of the Jewish Faith, and Jesus as the Jewish Messiah. They felt that entry into the Church was by way of the Jewish religion. Even Peter needed a special vision to impress upon him that people of every nation were acceptable (Acts 10). Paul was the apostle who had the clearest view of the Church's mission to Jew and Gentile alike.

155 · The Ascension

Mark 16¹⁹⁻²⁰. Luke 24⁴⁷⁻⁵³ (Acts 1¹⁻¹²)

The 'Epilogue' of Mark's Gospel makes very brief mention of the fact that Jesus was *received up into heaven*. Jesus wished to indicate to his disciples the finality of his departure. Since they thought that *upwards* was the direction of heaven, a dramatic visible ascent was the obvious way in which to help them realize that he had returned there. The cloud that intervened, and symbolized his entry into the divine glory, terminated the demonstration (Acts 1⁹).

The ascension story is not meant to make known the actual location of heaven. Perhaps in the twentieth century, instead of calling the commemoration of this event Ascension Day, although it was that for the disciples, it would be better to say Exaltation Day. This would be a reminder that when we use our inadequate human language to speak of God and Christ as 'up', 'high', or 'above', we use these terms not literally, but in the way in which we commonly do to denote priority, rank, position, or authority.

LUKE. Luke's fullest account of the ascension is kept for his second volume, the Acts of the Apostles. Luke 24^{47-53} is therefore an abridged version of Acts 1. His Gospel he concludes in the same setting as that in which it opens, the Temple. Some important manuscripts of Luke omit the words *and was carried up into heaven* (see R.V. margin).

Supplementary Articles

156 · The Gospel Miracles

The miracles recorded in the Gospels need to be regarded in a way very different from those in the Old Testament. The New Testament miracles were recorded in our Gospels within the living memory of those who had known Jesus directly. The accounts of the Old Testament miracles were not written down for centuries after the incidents alleged. During that time details became elaborated, and marvels became more marvellous. Moreover, quite natural events would appear as miracles to primitive minds, which saw the power of God in everything.

Many people find the New Testament miracles difficult to accept. Some therefore try to remove from the life of Jesus, as it is outlined in the Gospels, all the miracles and other mentions of the supernatural. Others try to explain these parts away. The following points should be borne in mind:

(1) The supreme miracle of the Christian Faith is that God became a human being. If one believes that this happened, and Christians claim that it did, by comparison all other miracles become possible, for God himself is directly at work in the world. It has been said that we do not believe in Jesus because of the miracles, but in the miracles because we believe in Jesus.

(2) In the temptations in the wilderness, Jesus refused to undertake miracles to attract attention. He always regarded them as secondary to his teaching (Mark 1³⁴⁻³⁸, 2¹⁰).

(3) The purpose of the miracles was to show various aspects of Jesus' power, over disease, the spirit world, death, etc. The miracles are rightly described in the Fourth Gospel as 'signs', signs that the power of God in Jesus was at work in the world.

(4) The number of miracles recorded is actually few. An impressive feature is the matter-of-fact way in which they are described: there is very little striving after dramatic effect; the astonishment of onlookers receives only casual mention. This restraint on the part of the Gospel

writers is in marked contrast to the fanciful wonders of other writers of their time.

(5) It is a mistake to imagine that people living two thousand years ago were unintelligent and easily deceived. Some of those still reckoned among the world's greatest thinkers lived even earlier still. The disciples of Jesus were quite as capable as we are of knowing what was normally impossible. It is worth remembering that the total consecutive lives of no more than thirty men would bridge the gap between their time and ours.

(6) It is sometimes said that miracles are contrary to the laws of nature. This presupposes that the laws of nature are all already known. Miracles are certainly contrary to any known laws. Perhaps the laws of nature that Jesus used may one day be discovered, or perhaps the miracles really were the results of God's direct intervention in the ordinary course of things.

(7) Details of a few Gospel miracles may have got altered in the telling, but this does not require that all the other miracles need be doubted.

157 · The Resurrection

(1) If, as Christians believe, God himself entered the world in the person of Jesus, the resurrection is quite logical, for death could not be stronger than God. There is no point in denying the resurrection because people do not usually rise from the dead: God's entering the world was something unique; so too would be a resurrection.

(2) Christians believe that Jesus lived a perfect human life (Hebrews 4¹⁵). If he did not rise from the dead, good was beaten by evil, and that is harder to believe.

(3) Something tremendous must have happened to change the frightened disciples into missionaries ready to face death for the truth of their statements.

(4) The resurrection made such an impact upon the disciples that it became the central theme of their teaching (1 Corinthians 15¹⁴). Whether or not Jesus rose from the dead, the first Christians were sure that he did.

(5) Various theories have been put forward to explain the resurrection in a non-literal sense:

(a) It has been suggested that Jesus did not die upon the cross, and that he recovered in the tomb. The suggestion ignores the testimony of the centurion on duty (Mark 15⁴⁴⁻⁴⁵) and the statement in the

Fourth Gospel that Jesus' side was pierced by a spear (John 19$^{33-34}$). It also ignores the difficulty of opening the tomb from the inside and appearing strong and healthy.

(b) Another suggestion is that the women went to the wrong tomb, and that some young man in white redirected them. The women were then too frightened to continue, and later, when rumours of Jesus' reappearance arose, connected them with their own experience. The suggestion ignores the repeated statement in the Gospels that the women knew the tomb already.

(c) Discrepancies in the resurrection stories cause some people to doubt them. But the discrepancies are comparatively slight, and are far more an indication of truth than would be complete agreement. Newspapers illustrate this daily.

(d) Too many disciples of Jesus saw him alive for hallucination to be any answer (I Corinthians 15$^{3-8}$). People who have hallucinations are already in a receptive state of mind. The disciples were not: they had recently buried their master, and were not expecting to see him alive. His predictions about his future had never made much impression. The appearance of precision in the records may well be due to their being made after the actual events.

(e) The suggestion that the disciples stole the body is one that did not arise in Palestine (see Section 148). Bodies are not easy to conceal, and Caiaphas and the chief priests must have done their best to find this one. Someone, to gain a possible reward, would surely have come forward with information. Moreover, Caiaphas never said that the story of Jesus' resurrection was false: all that he could do was to threaten the disciples to make them keep silent about it (Acts 3–5).

People are often puzzled by the nature of the resurrection appearances. It is clear that Jesus was neither a ghostly apparition, nor exactly the same physical human being that he had been. Nor was he only a vision, for the disciples were physically, not spiritually, aware of his presence. His risen body was such that the disciples could touch it, and he could eat food to help convince them.

Some may wonder where Jesus was when he was not appearing to his disciples. It has been suggested that Jesus' ascension took place immediately after his resurrection, and that his words to Mary Magdalene are an indication of this (John 20$^{17-18}$). It seems reasonable that when his triumph over death was complete he should at once return whence he had come.

If this was so, then Jesus, having returned on the first Easter Day to the spiritual realms of glory, for several weeks thereafter made frequent visits into the human sphere in order to strengthen the faith of his disciples, and possibly to give them further guidance. In this case, Ascension Day becomes the commemoration of Jesus' last and most dramatic transition from the earthly to the heavenly realm.

158 · The Kingdom of God

A prominent subject in all Jesus' teaching was the kingdom of God. To understand what he meant by this phrase it is necessary to consider what it meant already to the people who heard him.

(1) *Political*

Although God was the creator of the whole world, and therefore in the widest sense its King, the Jews regarded him as their King in particular, inasmuch as God was believed to have entered into a special covenant with them. In this respect God's kingdom was the Jewish nation, for it was the Jewish people who acknowledged his sovereignty. The Jewish nation was a theocracy; even her kings, unlike oriental despots, did not claim absolute power, but regarded themselves as God's vice-regents, the Lord's Anointed Ones, and answerable to him.

(2) *Religious*

The more the Jewish people suffered at the hands of their enemies, the greater grew their longing for a Day of the Lord, wherein God would vindicate himself and them, and by means of his Messiah would establish the kingdom in its fulness.

In the Teaching of Jesus

When Jesus used the phrase 'kingdom of God' he used it in two ways:

(1) *The Future.* Jesus' teaching seems to indicate that he too, like other Jews, saw the kingdom of God in the future, when the Son of man would come with the angels, and *gather together his elect from the four winds.* After judgement, and the end of all things, the kingdom would be finally complete and perfect. In heaven would be the Messianic banquet, spurned by those first invited, but attended by the despised and outcast. In heaven would be the wise virgins, the separated sheep, the wheat, and the selected fish.

(2) *The Present.* Jesus made to the idea of the kingdom an entirely new contribution. He taught that the kingdom had come already, not in a political sense, but spiritually, in the hearts of all who accepted God's sovereignty (Luke 17^{20-21}). Although the kingdom belonged

ultimately to heaven, it was also, by the coming of Jesus, spreading on earth.

Jews believed that the world was in the power of evil. Jesus was weakening its hold, and reclaiming the world for God, its rightful King. His acts of healing and exorcism were a demonstration of this (Matthew 12^{28}). Jesus taught his followers to pray that God's kingdom might come as in heaven so on earth, and regarded all who welcomed him as already members of that kingdom. It is not surprising, therefore, that the first Christians used the phrase 'kingdom of God' when referring to the Church.

In *Parables of the Kingdom* C. H. Dodd suggests that 'the kingdom of God has come' was the main theme of Jesus' teaching, and the particular truth embodied in the parables. The selection in many of them represented people's response to him. Their association with the future was due to early Christian interpretation.

159 · Teaching in Parables

Jesus, in common with all Jewish rabbis, often taught in parables. A parable is a comparison. It can be but a simile, a short saying that something is like something else: e.g. *The kingdom of heaven is like unto treasure*. Or it can be a complete story, such as The Good Samaritan.

Reasons for teaching in parables are:

(1) A story holds attention, illustrates an idea being taught, and helps to recall the idea to mind. (2) A parable is a challenge to the hearers. Involuntarily they think about it, and pass judgement upon it. So Jesus could put a question as in Luke 10^{36}.

In Mark 4$^{10-12}$, Matthew 13$^{10-17, 34-35}$, and Luke 8$^{9-10}$, are some rather puzzling words about Jesus' reason. They seem to imply a deliberate attempt by him to confuse his hearers, and to hide the truth away. All this seems most unlike the methods employed by Jesus in his teaching: it was because he spoke in terms that could be understood that people listened, and compared him favourably to the scribes.

What then is the explanation? Two explanations are possible. One is that despite Jesus' plain teaching there were those Jews who would not respond to it. There would always be people who would not make the least effort to understand. Here Jesus in irony is recalling words of God to the prophet Isaiah at the time of his call (Isaiah 6$^{9-10}$), where the result is stated as though it were the intention. A second explanation is that the words are a comment by the writers of the Gospels. At the time when they wrote, considerable opposition was experienced by

Christians when preaching to Jews. The words of God to Isaiah seemed to be true for Christians also. It was as though the Jews deliberately shut their eyes, ears, and hearts, to the truth. That some addition has here been made to the records is indicated by the question put by the disciples. Jews were too familiar with the parable method to be likely to ask Jesus why he used it.

Many scholars hold that the meanings given to the parables of The Tares, The Dragnet and The Sower, in the Gospels, are not explanations given by Jesus, but more likely are early Christian sermons upon the parables, reflecting Gentile interest in the details of a story, and so treating the parables as though they were allegories.

A remarkable thing about the parables is that they are so timeless. Applied to any age or situation, they are found to have a message. It is sometimes necessary to ask what was the original message. It may not have been the same as what we understand today. A certain traditional interpretation has developed through centuries of Church teaching.

Few of the parables have a fixed place in the narrative. Most of them therefore are grouped together in the following sections.

160 · Parables of the Kingdom

These are introduced by such words as *The kingdom of heaven is like unto . . .*

(1) *The Seed Growing Secretly* Mark 4$^{26-29}$

Here is a parable of hidden growth. It is likely that when Jesus told it he was teaching that the kingdom had already come. The seed of the kingdom had been slowly growing throughout Jewish history. Now all was ready for Jesus to harvest the result.

For the first Christians the parable described the spread of Christianity during the period between the ascension and the second advent. Jesus' coming seemed long delayed, but the parable suggested the reason: although nothing appeared to be happening the harvest was on its way, and Jesus the Great Harvester would appear in due time. In a wider field this is still the interpretation today.

(2) *The Mustard Seed* Mark 4$^{30-32}$, Luke 13$^{18-19}$, Matthew 13$^{31-32}$

This is a parable about rapid growth. 'Small as a grain of mustard seed' was a Jewish proverb. Yet from very small beginnings the mustard seed can, in a short time, grow into a shrub as much as six feet high. It is probable that when Jesus first told the parable he wished to point out that the kingdom had come, and, like a mustard tree, was already casting its shadow for those who wished to shelter under its branches (cf. Daniel 4$^{12, 21}$, Ezekiel 17^{23}, 31^6).

For the first Christians the parable would speak of the rapid growth of the kingdom in their own age of missionary activity. They regarded the spread of the Christian religion as a matter of great urgency, for the Christian community was the mustard seed of the kingdom, and that must be fully grown before the expected early return of Jesus.

(3) *The Leaven* Luke 13$^{20-21}$, Matthew 13^{33}

This is a parable about transforming power. Leaven or yeast could be symbolic of either a good or a bad influence (cf. Mark 8^{15}). It is likely that, when Jesus told this parable, he was thinking of how the power of God had been at work in Jewish history almost unobtrusively. Now, in his own ministry, the power of God was transforming Judaism visibly.

The first Christians would apply the parable to the power of the Holy Spirit active in the spread of Christianity, transforming not merely Judaism but the whole world.

(4) *The Tares* Matthew 13$^{24-30, 36-43}$

This parable is not unlike that of The Seed Growing Secretly, for the seed is sown, and the harvest awaited, but before it can be gathered a sorting out is required. Jesus was probably thinking here of the Jewish nation as the kingdom of God containing elements both good and bad. Jesus and his disciples were the reapers about to help the *wheat* sort itself from the *tares*.

The early Christian interpretation of the parable is found in vv. 36–43, which most scholars agree is not part of the original. Here the growing of wheat and tares together belongs not to Jewish history, but to the interval between the ascension of Jesus and his second advent.

(5) *The Hidden Treasure* Matthew 13^{44} (See below)

(6) *The Costly Pearl* Matthew 13$^{45-46}$

These two short parables have the same meaning: to gain admission to the kingdom it is worth while to give everything.

(7) *The Dragnet* Matthew 13$^{47-50}$

In this parable a fisherman sorts out his catch as a farmer does his harvest. Here possibly Jesus is thinking of himself and his disciples as fishers of men, checking what people qualify themselves to be in the kingdom.

But it is possible also that Jesus was here warning his disciples that, in their work for him, they would find unworthy as well as worthy men claiming membership of the kingdom. This was the meaning of the parable for the early Christians, and it is probably their interpretation that is found in vv. 49–50. In their view the sorting out of the good and bad within the kingdom would take place at the second advent and final judgement.

(8) *The Great Supper* Luke 14$^{15-24}$ (See below)

(9) *The Marriage Feast* Matthew 22$^{1-10}$

These parables are regarded by some scholars as variations of the same story. A banquet was a well-known symbol for the Messianic kingdom. This one reflects the Eastern custom whereby servants were sent out when a meal was ready to give a final courteous invitation.

When Jesus first told this parable he was probably thinking of the Jewish people as those to whom God had given, and was still giving, special opportunities, and of himself as saying, *Come; for all things are now ready*. For the first Christians the parable would describe how the Jews had rejected Jesus, and how they themselves were now inviting all kinds of people to the banquet that would follow the second advent (cf. Acts 13^{46}).

(10) *The Labourers in the Vineyard* Matthew 20$^{1-16}$

The keynote of this parable is generosity. The generous employer gave a full day's wage (a denarius) to those who worked only a short time: it was not their fault that they had remained so long unemployed.

When Jesus told the parable he was no doubt describing the generosity of God, who was calling all and sundry into his kingdom. From the time of Isaiah, however, a vineyard had been a symbol for Israel. The first Christians, therefore, tended to identify the late-comers with the late-comers among themselves (Gentile converts) and to find in the parable a lesson that God's blessings are not qualified for by personal merit or length of service.

(11) *The Ten Virgins* Matthew 25$^{1-13}$

This is a parable about watchfulness. The scene is a Palestinian wedding, during which a bridegroom went in procession to the bride's house, and, after much festivity, conducted her back to his own. It is not clear in the parable whether the ten virgins are at the bride's house, awaiting the bridegroom's arrival there, or at his house, waiting to welcome him back again with his bride. Some scholars suggest that the *virgins* were male attendants, because females would not go to shops

L

late at night (cf. Revelation 14⁴, and the parable of The Waiting Servants, Luke 12³⁵⁻⁴⁰, which is reminiscent of this one).

When Jesus first told the parable he may well have been commenting on the fact that many Jews were unprepared for the coming of their Messiah. He was himself the Messianic bridegroom. In effect John the Baptist had proclaimed him as such. In these circumstances the wise virgins were those entering the kingdom with him. There is a note of urgency in the parable: those who are unprepared may soon find it too late.

The first Christians saw the parable as one of readiness for the second advent. Hence the comment, *Watch therefore, for ye know not the day nor the hour.* That is why Matthew puts the parable immediately after Jesus' teaching about the second advent.

(12) *The Unmerciful Servant* Matthew 18²¹⁻³⁵

According to the rabbis, forgiveness seven times over was sufficient, for seven was the symbol of completeness. As Jesus taught the parable, however, it meant that those who wished to belong to the kingdom must act towards others as generously as God had towards them.

161 · Parables about the Kingdom

There is a number of parables about the kingdom, although they are not directly introduced as such.

(1) *The Wedding Garment* Matthew 22¹¹⁻¹⁴

This parable occurs as a sequel to The Marriage Feast. Most scholars believe it to have been originally a separate parable, because a guest brought in unexpectedly from the highway could scarcely be blamed for not wearing a wedding garment.

As a separate parable, however, its teaching is still very much like that of The Marriage Feast. In that parable those first invited made excuses, and did not go; in this, one of the guests attended the feast but insulted his host by not coming properly prepared. The parable is similar to one told by Jewish rabbis, in which some invited guests were ready dressed when the call came, and some were not.

The overall teaching is that many Jews were not interested in, nor prepared for, the kingdom. The first Christians would see the parable as a warning always to be ready for the second advent.

(2) *The Talents.* Matthew 25¹⁴⁻³⁰

The parable follows that of The Ten Virgins, which is introduced as a parable of the kingdom. The servant who *hid his lord's money* is condemned for his idleness, and rebuked for trying to divert blame from himself by finding fault with his master as being a hard business man scarcely deserving of further gain.

When Jesus first told the parable he was probably thinking about the Jewish people to whom God had entrusted so much in the way of revelation. This they should have been more ready to spread among other people. Now they ran the risk of losing their opportunity. The first Christians looked upon the day of reckoning as representing the second advent, when the faithful would be rewarded for the good use that they had made of God's favours. This is why Matthew has placed the parable after Jesus' teaching about the end of all things.

(3) *The Pounds* Luke 19¹¹⁻²⁸

This parable has much in common with The Talents: the details are different, but the main contents are the same. Jesus no doubt told his parables many times over, and, though teaching the same lessons, made variations in the composition of the parables.

The main difference here is that in The Talents the servants are given money in accordance with their varying ability: in The Pounds each is given the same amount.

(4) *The Servants Watching* Luke 12³⁵⁻³⁸

This parable is not unlike that of The Ten Virgins. The main difference is that those awaiting the bridegroom's arrival are men-servants. The long delay is emphasized by mention of the varying night watches, 9–12, 12–3, 3–6, Jewish reckoning.

The message of the parable, like that of The Ten Virgins, is watchfulness for the coming of the Son of man, both his first coming, and, as the Christians interpreted it, his second (see Mark 13³³⁻³⁷).

(5) *The Thief at Night* Luke 12³⁹⁻⁴⁰, Matthew 24⁴³⁻⁴⁴

This is another parable with watchfulness as the theme. Just as his first coming had caught many Jews unprepared, so would the second.

(6) *The Faithful or Unfaithful Steward* Luke 12⁴¹⁻⁴⁸, Matthew 24⁴⁵⁻⁵¹

In Luke this parable appears as an answer to a question put by Peter. It is another parable about servants in their master's absence. When Jesus first told the parable he was probably thinking of the Jewish people as betraying the trust that God had placed in them.

The first Christians applied the parable to the Christian community. In particular they saw it as a solemn reminder to those in any office not to misuse their authority. When the second advent came, the unfaithful *stewards of the mysteries of God*, as St. Paul described them, would receive harsh judgement. Other Christians would be judged according to how far they realized that they had disobeyed their Master's will.

(7) *The Unjust Steward* Luke 16$^{1-13}$

In this parable, unlike the other parables about servants, the master does not go away. The varying amounts of the reductions may have been designed to conceal the steward's device. His master commended him because he acted wisely (or prudently) not because he did right. In v. 8 the Greek has 'the lord', which makes it possible to argue that the commendation came from Jesus, but this does not accord with the emphatic *and I* in v. 9, and has been rejected by the translators of the Revised Version.

When Jesus first told the parable he may possibly have been thinking of the leaders of the Jewish nation, reluctant to acknowledge the coming of the kingdom, and playing safe for themselves with the Romans. Alternatively, since the parable was spoken *unto the disciples* (as compared with the Pharisees and scribes in 15$^{2-3}$), Jesus may have been giving a particular warning to Judas, regarding his secret misuse of the money in his charge. Nevertheless the Pharisees *heard all these things* (16^{14}).

V. 9 has two possible meanings. The *mammon of unrighteousness* meant worldly wealth. One possible meaning is therefore, 'use your worldly wealth in order to do good, and so make friends who will stand by you when it shall fail' (or 'when you die', say some manuscripts). A second suggestion is that, instead of 'by means of the mammon of unrighteousness', the Greek means 'out of the mammon of unrighteousness' (R.V. margin), or rather 'apart from'. This gives a meaning, 'make friends apart from considerations of wealth or influence, for these are the friends who will remain true when wealth shall fail. These friends will be ready to welcome you into the next world.'

Both meanings say in effect, 'Faithfulness over the stewardship of this world's goods is a wise preparation for heavenly riches.'

(8) *The Sower* Mark 4$^{1-9, 13-20}$, Matthew 13$^{1-9, 18-23}$, Luke 8$^{4-8, 11-15}$

This parable, although not specifically introduced as a parable of the kingdom, is nevertheless one of growth, and as such has much in common with The Tares, The Mustard Seed, and The Seed Growing Secretly. Like them it proclaimed that the kingdom had come, although all were not ready for it. Thus Jesus, when telling the parable, may well have been thinking of himself and his disciples as reapers about to gather into the kingdom the harvest of Israel, and finding gaps in the harvest field where such as the scribes and Pharisees should have been.

The interpretation, as given in the Gospels, is felt by many scholars not to be the work of Jesus. Instead of treating the details of the story as merely background, the interpretation treats them as allegory, with each having a specific meaning. This treatment belongs more to Gentile than to Jewish thought.

The explanation, as given, is such as Gentile Christians would appreciate. Thus the preaching of Jesus is represented as the work of sowing the Word, rather than as reaping results, and the harvest is in the future. The interpretation reveals the environment in which the first Christians lived. When Mark wrote the parable in his Gospel for Roman Christians to read, many, including Peter and Paul, had recently died as martyrs in the Neronian persecution. The parable therefore might well be used as an exhortation to steadfastness.

(9) *The Lost Sheep* Luke 15$^{1-7}$, Matthew 18$^{12-13}$ (See below)

(10) *The Lost Coin* Luke 15$^{8-10}$

These two parables illustrate God's concern for 'the lost', the one a sheep, lost through its foolishness, the other a coin, lost through no fault of its own. In the case of the lost sheep the hearers of Jesus would at once think in terms of God as the Shepherd of Israel. The Lost Coin would be one of ten worn by women on a cord around the forehead.

In these parables Jesus was describing his mission to the *lost sheep of the house of Israel*, i.e. the publicans and sinners.

Luke adds a comment about rejoicing in heaven. This may seem somewhat inappreciative of people quietly living good lives, but the emphasis in both parables is on recovery, rather than upon not getting lost.

(11) *The Prodigal Son* Luke 15$^{11-32}$

This is another parable of God's concern for the lost. It is sometimes given two additional titles, The Father, and The Elder Brother. Again there is the lost, the seeker, and the rejoicing. But here the son is lost through his own deliberate action, unlike the unintelligent sheep, and the inanimate coin, and his elder brother comes more prominently into the picture than do the static sheep and coins. Both sons have good qualities, and both bad.

The younger son would get a third of his father's property. Jews did not keep pigs. So feeding them represented degradation.

When Jesus told the parable he was again thinking of his mission to bring publicans and sinners into the kingdom. They were the 'lost son'. The jealous elder brother represented the disdainful scribes and Pharisees.

SUPPLEMENTARY ARTICLES

(12) *The Two Sons* Matthew 21²⁸⁻³²

This parable is reminiscent of the parable of The Two Foundations, which ends the Sermon on the Mount (Matthew 7²⁴⁻²⁷). In both the emphasis is on the importance of *doing*.

Jesus was thinking of the Pharisees, who paid only lip service to their religion, and of the publicans and sinners who were prepared actually to repent and to enter the kingdom.

(13) *The Chief Seats* Luke 14⁷⁻¹⁴

This parable is concerned with humility. The humble person does not push himself forward. Yet a marriage feast or banquet was a symbol of the Messianic kingdom. Jesus may therefore have been thinking particularly of those Jews who assumed that they were naturally entitled to the best places in it.

162 · General Parables

(1) *The Pharisee and the Publican* Luke 18⁹⁻¹⁴

This is a parable about humility in prayer. The publican was justified in that his manner of praying was acceptable.

(2) *The Unjust Judge* Luke 18¹⁻⁸

This is a parable about the need for perseverance in prayer. With it should be compared the Sermon on the Mount, Matthew 7⁷⁻¹¹, and the parable of The Friend at Midnight, Luke 11⁵⁻⁸.

(3) *The Rich Fool* Luke 12¹³⁻²¹

This parable is a warning against covetousness and avarice. The same teaching occurs in the Sermon on the Mount (Matthew 6¹⁹⁻²¹).

(4) *The Rich Man and Lazarus* Luke 16¹⁴⁻¹⁵, ¹⁹⁻³¹

This is a parable about the misuse of wealth. It was not wrong for the rich man to be wealthy, but wrong for him to be oblivious of those in need. His wealth, moreover, led him to self-indulgence. He is sometimes called Dives, a Latin word meaning rich. Lazarus was a common name.

The parable is not intended to give a description of life in the next world, though it is an indication of the reality of an after-life. *Abraham's bosom, this flame*, and the *great gulf*, were all well-known picture language. *Lazarus in Abraham's bosom* meant that he was reclining next to Abraham in the celestial banquet. The last verse would later echo significantly in the ears of Christian missionaries.

(5) *The Sheep and the Goats* Matthew 25³¹⁻⁴⁶

This is sometimes thought to be not so much a parable as a Christian apocalypse, or sermon about judgement, but even so it must be regarded as containing actual teaching of Jesus. The idea of the Son of man coming in judgement upon all nations is borrowed from the Old Testament book of Daniel, and the Apocryphal book of Enoch.

Those who received a reward were *doers*, not merely hearers. Jesus often pointed out that the way to true greatness was by service to others, and cited himself as an example (cf. the parables of The Two Foundations and The Two Sons).

(6) *The Tower Builder* Luke 14²⁵⁻³⁰ (See below)

(7) *The King Going to War* Luke 14³¹⁻³³

These are parables about the cost of discipleship. Jesus did not mean that a follower of his must hate his family, but that, if there were a conflict of loyalties, his own claim must have priority. Even life itself might have to be forfeited.

It was well to consider all this, and count the cost, before professing discipleship.

(8) *The Unprofitable Servant* Luke 17⁷⁻¹⁰

This parable is a reminder that those who serve God faithfully are giving him no more than his due. It would be impossible to give to God anything that it was not his right to expect. Conversely, any rewards given by God are acts of generosity on his part.

(9) *Parables Dealt with elsewhere*

	section
The Two Debtors	65
The Good Samaritan	120
The Friend at Midnight	56
The Fruitless Fig Tree	115
The Two Foundations	60
New Cloth and New Wine	39
The Wicked Husbandmen	117
The Fig Tree and all the Trees	124
The Splinter and the Beam	54
The Unclean Spirits	66

163 · The Son of Man

This is the title that Jesus used most frequently for himself. In the New Testament, apart from one exception in Acts 7[56], it appears in this form only in the Gospels. To understand why Jesus chose the title as being appropriate it is necessary to trace its history in the Old Testament.

(1) *Psalm* 8[4–5]

What is man, that thou art mindful of him? And the son of man that thou visitest him? This verse from the psalm is a typical example of Hebrew poetry, where the second line repeats the thoughts expressed in the first. Here *son of man* in the second line is but a poetic repetition of *man* in the first.

The psalm continues: *For thou hast made him but little lower than God, and crownest him with glory and honour.* Though the Psalmist uses the phrase *son of man* to mean no more than mankind in general, yet two important ideas are expressed in these two verses: man in his lowliness and insignificance as God's creation, and man's possibility of glory.

(2) *Ezekiel*

The phrase *son of man* gains a little more meaning when used in the book of Ezekiel, God uses the title when he speaks to Ezekiel. Indeed Ezekiel is addressed as *son of man* more than ninety times. The phrase still means *man*, but also there is a suggestion of something more, for Ezekiel as a prophet was called to be God's representative to his people, and the people's representative before God. God made him responsible for them.

(3) *Daniel*

A use of the phrase still more significant occurs in Daniel 7[13–14]. V. 27 explains that the mysterious being represents *the people of the saints of the Most High*, i.e. the faithful community of Israel. Thus in Daniel the *son of man* is a personification of faithful Israel.

(4) *Other Jewish Literature*

Jewish literature, apart from the Old Testament, develops the idea in Daniel yet further. The Son of man is a supernatural being who existed before the creation of sun and stars. He is destined to be the judge of men and angels, and to reign for ever.

It is easy to see why this title Son of man appealed to Jesus. He combined the ideas behind it with those of the Suffering Servant described in the Servant Songs (Isaiah 42$^{1-4}$, 49$^{1-6}$, 50$^{4-9}$, 52^{13}-53^{12}). The Suffering Servant like the *son of man* in Psalm 8 was to be humbled, and then to be exalted by God. Thus Jesus used the title for himself in a very distinctive way: (*a*) When speaking of his own forthcoming humiliation and suffering (Mark 8^{31}, 9^9, 9^{31}, 10$^{33, 45}$, 14^{62}). Here the title is linked with the idea of the Suffering Servant. (*b*) When speaking of his forthcoming exaltation and glory (Mark 13^{26}, Matthew 25^{31}, Luke 21^{36}). Here Jesus is thinking of the Son of man as described in Daniel, and of the Son of man who will come to judge angels and men.

In addition to the obvious appropriateness of this title, Jesus had another good reason for using it. The title Messiah, especially in the early stages of his ministry, would have been a dangerous one to use, and likely to cause misunderstanding. On the other hand Son of man was ambiguous. It is possible that in the time of Jesus it could be used to mean Messiah, but it could also mean no more than Man, as in Psalm 8. Jesus himself occasionally used it in this non-committal way (Mark 2^{28}). Sometimes he used it instead of the pronoun I (Luke 9^{58}).

Jesus used the title most after Peter's Confession at Caesarea Philippi. This was a turning-point in his ministry. As the Twelve recognized him as the Messiah, so he became more aware of himself as the Suffering Servant.

164 · Son of God

This title, like that of Son of man, has a long Jewish history behind it, but unlike that title is not used directly by Jesus in the Synoptic Gospels.

Because the Jews as a nation thought of God as a Father, they regarded themselves as 'sons of God'. Moses, speaking on God's behalf to Pharaoh, said *Israel is my son, my firstborn* (Exodus 4^{22}). (See also Psalms 68^5, 82^6, 103$^{1-13}$, Isaiah 1^2, Jeremiah 31^9, Hosea 11^1, Malachi 2^{10}). It was not unusual for Jewish prayers to address God as 'Our Father in Heaven'.

The idea of God as a Father resulted in individuals also being regarded as his sons or children: (*a*) Angelic beings (Genesis 6$^{1-4}$, Job 1^6, 38^7, Psalm 29^1); (*b*) Kings (II Samuel 7^{14}); (*c*) Righteous people (Matthew 5^9, Mark 15^{39} R.V. margin).

It is possible that in the time of Jesus the phrase Son of God was used with special significance for the expected Messiah, since the high priest asked Jesus, *Art thou the Christ, the Son of the Blessed?* (Mark 14^{61}). (Note also Matthew 16^{16}, 27^{40}.)

In the New Testament the title Son of God is one given to Jesus by his followers. (Jesus does not describe himself in this way except in the

M

Fourth Gospel, which is a theological meditation rather than a biography.) When the first Christians used the title for Jesus it implied more than it had ever done in previous Jewish use. Christians believed that Jesus was the Son of God in a unique and personal way, and so divine.

Some scholars contend that the first Christians fabricated the divinity of Jesus for him. It is true that the Synoptic Gospels contain few mentions of Jesus as the Son of God in any special sense, and that some of the occasions may be due to the fact that the Gospels were written by people looking back upon things, and using language that had later become current among themselves (e.g. Matthew 14[33]). But if the divinity of Jesus were fabricated by the first Christians, it was a fabrication for which hundreds of them were prepared to give their lives.

Authentic, and therefore significant, passages are:

(1) Mark 1[11], 9[7]. Perhaps only Jesus heard the voice, and perhaps that only in his mind, but the phrase twice repeated shows his own conviction.

(2) Luke 10[22] (and Matthew 11[27]). These words come from document Q. Here Jesus was conscious of having a unique relationship with God as his Father: only he fully knew God; only he therefore could reveal God to men.

It was Jesus' own conviction of himself as God's Son that convinced his followers, the first of whom were Jews brought up in the firm belief that *God is One*. It is remarkable that, by the time that Matthew's Gospel was written, a community of people brought up in such belief, could accept baptism in the name of Father, Son, and Holy Spirit (Matthew 28[19]). And long before this, indeed within five years of the resurrection, Paul, formerly a strict Pharisee, was preaching in the synagogues *that he is the Son of God* (Acts 9[20]).

165 · Chief Jewish Parties

The Sadducees

This was a party of wealthy and aristocratic priests. Their name is probably derived from Zadok, the priest who anointed Solomon (I Kings 1[39]). Though not so numerous as the Pharisees, the Sadducees were much more influential. In the time of Jesus, the high priest Caiaphas and the chief priests were Sadducees. They saw the advantages of co-operating with Rome.

The Sadducees upheld the authority of the Law of Moses, but not the traditions of the scribes, nor did they believe in angels, spirits, or any after life. This meant that they took particular exception to the disciples' preaching that Jesus had risen from the dead. On this same matter Paul cleverly set Sadducees against Pharisees when they met to accuse him (Acts 23$^{6-9}$).

The Pharisees

Unlike the Sadducees, Pharisees regarded the traditions of the scribes as of equal importance with the actual Law; they believed in angels, life after death, and a coming judgement.

Their name means 'separated ones'. They were the successors of the 'pious ones', a group of Jews who, after the Greek invasion of Palestine by Alexander the Great, refused to be influenced by the introduction of Greek ideas and culture. They believed that the only way to preserve Judaism was to maintain complete separation from all Gentiles. When the Greek king Antiochus Epiphanes tried to eliminate Judaism, many 'pious ones' died as martyrs.

By the time of Jesus, Pharisaic zeal for the Law and the traditions had become an end in itself. Their separateness then became, not merely that of Jew from Gentile, but of Pharisees from fellow Jews who did not have the same scrupulous regard for legal details as themselves.

The Pharisees, together with the scribes, are frequently mentioned in the Gospels for their opposition to Jesus. They objected to his attitude towards the ceremonial law, and to his association with those who neglected the Law and their own principle of exclusiveness.

The Scribes or Lawyers

The scribes were 'writers'. Their great predecessor was Ezra (Ezra 7^{10}). It was their work to copy out the Jewish Scriptures. They thus became learned in the Law of Moses, and acquired authority to interpret it. Many scribes were Pharisees.

The Herodians

These formed a political party which supported the dynasty of Herod and the rule of Rome. They were noted for their religious indifference, and low morals. Normally the opponents of the Pharisees, the Herodians combined with them in their campaign against Jesus.

Scripture passages indexed to sections

MATTHEW

Index

Subject matter indexed to pages